MW00811685

Kabbalah

Unlocking Hermetic Qabalah to Understand Jewish Mysticism and Kabbalistic Rituals, Ideas, and History

Free Bonus from Silvia Hill available for limited time

Hi Spirituality Lovers!

My name is Silvia Hill, and first off, I want to THANK YOU for reading my book.

Now you have a chance to join my exclusive spirituality email list so you can get the ebooks below for free as well as the potential to get more spirituality ebooks for free! Simply click the link below to join.

P.S. Remember that it's 100% free to join the list.

~~$27~~ FREE BONUSES

- 👐 9 Types of Spirit Guides and How to Connect to Them
- 👐 How to Develop Your Intuition: 7 Secrets for Psychic Development and Tarot Reading
- 👐 Tarot Reading Secrets for Love, Career, and General Messages

Access your free bonuses here
https://livetolearn.lpages.co/kabbalah-paperback/

Table of Contents

Introduction

Have you ever wondered what the Tree of Life is? Or what is Kabbalah all about? If so, this book is for you!

Kabbalah - a way of thinking and being spiritual that has grown from Judaism - teaches about the divine nature of the universe, how people relate to God, and how to grow and find spiritual fulfillment. Despite its ancient origins, Kabbalah is not just for Jews - it is a system of thought and universal knowledge that can be studied and practiced by people of any religion or background.

The term "Kabbalah" is derived from the Hebrew root word "to receive," which refers to the act of receiving divine knowledge. Kabbalah is often called a "mystical" tradition and has some mysteries and secrets. But at its core, Kabbalah is a practical system that can improve your life and relationships and help you find meaning and purpose in the world.

The concepts and symbolism of Kabbalah can be found echoed in many different cultures and religions, including Christianity, Islam, and Buddhism. It has recently become increasingly popular in the West, especially as well-known celebrities have voiced their interest in the system. While Kabbalah has been gaining popularity, there is still a lot of misunderstanding about what it is.

Most people think of Kabbalah as a form of magic or witchcraft, *but this is incorrect.* It's not about performing spells or rituals; it is a system of thought that can be used to understand and interpret the world around us. Kabbalah is often linked to the Jewish mystical tradition, but it is not just for Jews; Kabbalah is a *universal system that people of any background or religion can study and practice.*

This book begins with an introduction to the basics of Kabbalah, including its history and practical applications. We'll discuss who can become a Kabbalist, the Tree of Life, and what it has to do with the belief system. Then, we'll explore some of the critical concepts of Kabbalah, such as the Sephirot and the 22 paths. You'll also learn about the different worlds of Kabbalah and how to apply Kabbalistic principles to your everyday life.

By the end of this book, you will better understand what Kabbalah is (and isn't) and how you can use its teachings to improve your life. You will also learn how to bring Kabbalistic ideas into your everyday life through rituals and practices to make you feel more peaceful, clear-thinking, and aware of yourself. Whether you are new to Kabbalah or want to learn more about this ancient system of thought, this book is the perfect introduction.

Chapter 1: A Brief History of Kabbalah

Kabbalah is a Hebrew term that means "to receive" or "receiver." This refers to the act of receiving knowledge or wisdom from a source outside of the individual. There are many different spellings of the word Kabbalah, such as Qabalah or Cabbalah. However, the most commonly used one is Kabbalah. No matter the tradition, this spelling will be used throughout the book to keep things clear.

The Star of David.
https://commons.wikimedia.org/wiki/File:V08p252001_Mizrach.jpg

This chapter will discuss where Kabbalah came from and how Jewish mysticism, Hermeticism, and the Order of the Golden Dawn interpreted it. It's crucial to note that there is *no single correct interpretation* of Kabbalah. Instead, each tradition has its unique way of understanding and using knowledge. Readers are encouraged to study each tradition and find the one that resonates with them the most.

What Is Kabbalah?

Mystics "...want to taste the whole wheat of spirit before it is ground by the millstones of reason." ~ Abraham Joshua

Kabbalah is a system of Jewish mysticism and magic that includes ideas and practices from many different sources, including the Bible, the Talmud, and ancient pagan traditions. Again, the word *Kabbalah* comes from the Hebrew word for "receiving," which refers to the idea that wisdom can be received from God or other spiritual beings. Kabbalistic beliefs and practices vary widely, but they involve studying biblical texts, meditating on mystical diagrams called "sefirot," and performing magical rituals.

Many Kabbalists also believe in reincarnation and the transmigration of souls. Kabbalah has affected many parts of Judaism, including how the Torah is read out loud in synagogues. Celebrities like Madonna and Britney Spears have also popularized it. While some Kabbalists believe their teachings should be kept secret, others have published books and created websites to share their beliefs with the world.

The Origins of Kabbalah

Kabbalah is a Jewish mysticism system that started taking shape in the 1200s. While it shares some commonalities with other mystical traditions, such as the belief in the existence of an unseen reality, Kabbalah also has a unique history and set of beliefs. One of the key figures in the development of Kabbalah was Isaac Luria, who taught that the universe had been created through a process of *tzimtzum*, or divine self-withdrawal. In Lurianic Kabbalah, God is seen as being inside and outside everything. Here on earth, people have the potential to work with God to make the world a better place. Kabbalah is still practiced by many Jews today as a way to get closer to

God and figure out what Jewish traditions are really about.

Early Origins

Kabbalah is thought to have started in ancient Babylonia, where Jewish mystics created a system of theosophy or divine wisdom. This system was later elaborated on by the rabbis of the Talmudic period. Kabbalah first began to develop as a distinct field of study in the 12th century in the Spanish city of Toledo. Ibn Gabirol's neo-Platonic philosophy and Ibn Arabi's Arabic mysticism influenced Jewish philosophers and mystics at this time. These thinkers attempted to synthesize Jewish tradition with the ideas of Plato and Aristotle.

The Zohar

The Zohar is the central text of the Kabbalah, a mystical tradition within Judaism. It is a book of allegorical stories and teachings meant to be interpreted on multiple levels. On a literal level, the Zohar tells the story of how the world was created and the fall of Adam and Eve. On a more spiritual level, it teaches about the nature of God, the relationship between man and God, and the path to salvation. The Zohar also provides insight into Jewish law and tradition. It is a very important piece of literature and a religious and spiritual teaching text. Its vivid stories and powerful images have been a source of ideas for artists and writers for hundreds of years. Kabbalists still study the Zohar today for what it says about religion and how well it is written.

Kabbalah in the Middle Ages

The Middle Ages were a time of great religious upheaval. With the rise of Christianity came the rise of new religious movements, including Kabbalah. Kabbalah teaches that God can be understood through mysterious symbols and hidden meanings. During the Middle Ages, the movement grew in popularity, especially among people who spoke Hebrew in Spain and Portugal. Even though the mainstream rabbinical establishment was skeptical of Kabbalah at first, it eventually won over many followers. Kabbalah greatly impacted Judaism, and its teachings still significantly impact both Judaism and Christianity today.

The 16th Century and Beyond

The Kabbalah says that the Torah has a hidden meaning; if people can figure out what it is, they can get closer to God. Kabbalists believe the Torah is like a tree, with each letter corresponding to a different branch or leaf. Kabbalists use many different methods, like gematria (*computing the numerical value of words*) and notarikon (*a cabalistic way of deriving a sentence from a single word*), to figure out the hidden meanings of the Torah. Once, only small groups of educated Jews were interested in Kabbalah. But recently, it has become more popular; celebrities and non-Jews are turning to its teachings for spiritual guidance.

In the 1600s, the Sabbatian crisis shook up the Jewish community. During this time, many Jews followed the false messiah, Sabbatai Zevi. He claimed to be the Jewish Messiah everyone had been waiting for, and his followers thought he would save them. But Zevi became a Muslim, which, understandably, made many of his followers lose faith in Kabbalah. In the 18th century, the Sabbatian crisis led to the start of the Hasidic movement. Hasidism sought to revive the spirituality of Kabbalah, and its followers believed that Kabbalah could help them achieve a close personal relationship with God. Hasidism is still an important part of Judaism, and its teachings have helped shape how people think about Kabbalah today.

Kabbalah in the Modern World

Kabbalah has experienced a renaissance in the modern world. Thanks to the work of thinkers like Rabbi Isaac Luria and Rabbi Moshe Cordovero, Kabbalah has been reintroduced to the mainstream Jewish community. Likewise, it is becoming more well-known among non-Jews who are simply interested in its mystical teachings and are drawn to Kabbalah's emphasis on personal spiritual growth. Its teachings have been featured in popular books like The Secret and The Da Vinci Code. As interest in Kabbalah continues to grow, its impact on the world will likely become even more pronounced.

Kabbalah in Jewish Mysticism

Kabbalah is a central component of Jewish mysticism. It is a tradition that says people can get close to God and talk with Him directly. *(Note: for consistency, we will use "Him" and "He" throughout this book, understanding that many believe God to be female or genderless.)* Kabbalah is based on the belief that there is a hidden meaning behind the Torah and that by understanding this hidden meaning, humans can achieve a personal connection with God. Kabbalists believe that the Torah is like a tree, with each letter corresponding to a different branch or leaf. As mentioned before, Kabbalists use many different methods to discover hidden meanings within the pages of the Torah.

Jewish mysticism has its roots in the ancient world. The first time Jewish mysticism is talked about in writing is in the book of Exodus when God gives Moses the Ten Commandments. Jewish mystics have tried to get to know God through prayer, meditation, and study for hundreds of years. In the Middle Ages, Kabbalah emerged as a major force in this quest for knowledge.

Kabbalah in Hermeticism

Hermeticism is a separate religious and philosophical tradition that also says people can have a personal relationship with God. Like Kabbalah, Hermeticism is based on the idea that the universe has a hidden meaning and that if people can figure out what it is, they can unlock its secrets. Based on principles from Hermes Trismegistus, it uses various methods to understand the hidden meaning of the universe. These methods include astrology, tarot, and numerology.

Hermeticism has its roots in the ancient world. The first recorded instance of hermeticism is found in the Emerald Tablet, a text purportedly written by the Egyptian god Hermes Trismegistus. Throughout the centuries, Hermetics have sought to experience the divine through magic, alchemy, and other esoteric practices. During the Renaissance, thinkers like Giordano Bruno and Cornelius Agrippa spread the ideas of Hermeticism, which became a major force in Western thought. In the modern world, hermeticism has experienced a resurgence in popularity, with people turning to its mystical teachings in search of guidance and spiritual enlightenment.

Kabbalah in The Order of the Golden Dawn

The Order of the Golden Dawn is a secret group that teaches its members how to do magic and get in touch with the divine in a personal way. Like the other belief systems, The Order is based on the belief that the universe has a hidden meaning and that humans can achieve a personal connection with the divine by understanding this hidden meaning. The Order of the Golden Dawn teaches its members how to use astrology, tarot, and numerology, among other things, to figure out what the universe is really all about.

The Order of the Golden Dawn has its roots in the Victorian era. In 1887, a group of British occultists who were interested in Hermeticism's magical teachings started the Order. It quickly became Britain's most influential secret society, with members like William Butler Yeats and Aleister Crowley carrying its teachings to the wider world. The Order of the Golden Dawn lost popularity in the 20th century, but its teachings have continued to influence occultists and mystics worldwide.

How Can We Learn from Any Tradition?

There's always something to learn from other cultures, whether it's their art, music, philosophical traditions, or simply the way they live their lives. One of the best ways to learn about another culture is to travel there and experience it first-hand. This can be difficult or impossible for some people, so another way to learn is to read about other cultures, watch documentaries, or even visit cultural centers or museums. Whichever method you choose, make sure you approach learning about other cultures with an open mind and a willingness to see things from a different perspective. Only then can you truly begin to understand and appreciate the beauty of diversity.

1. Do Not Take What Is Written as Truth

Many people think that they can only learn from their own traditions. However, this is not always the case. It's possible to learn from any tradition as long as we approach it with an open mind, curiosity, and a willingness to question what we read. When we take something at face value, we are more likely to blindly accept it as truth. However, when we critically engage with a tradition, we can learn a great deal by looking at its history, culture, and beliefs. In addition, by looking at a tradition through a critical lens, we can gain a deeper understanding of our own beliefs and traditions. So, the next time you hear about a new tradition, don't be afraid to ask questions and look at it closely. You may be surprised at what you learn.

2. Consider the Source

Countless traditions around the world have been passed down through generations. These traditions give us a window into the past and a connection to our heritage, from religious ceremonies to cultural customs. But as times change, some traditions may no longer be relevant or appropriate. So how can we learn from tradition without being bound by it?

One way to approach this is to consider the source of the tradition. Where did it come from, and why was it created? For example, many traditional gender roles were based on the idea that women were weaker and less capable than men. But now that we know better, we can question these outdated assumptions and create new traditions that are more equal and inclusive.

Another important thing to consider is whether the tradition is harmful in any way. Some traditions may seem harmless at first, but they may be sexist, racist, or homophobic when you look at them more closely. If a tradition is causing harm, an open discussion needs to be held about finding a remedy and how to implement it.

Finally, we should also be respectful of other cultures and their traditions. We can still learn from their customs and rituals even if we don't agree with everything they do. By doing so, we can create traditions that are more meaningful and relevant to our lives.

3. Study, Experiment, and Discern for Yourself

One of the great things about traditions is that they connect us to the past. They can offer us a sense of stability and belonging in a world that sometimes feels uncertain. However, traditions are not static; they evolve to meet the needs of those who practice them. If we want to learn from tradition, we need to be willing to study it. We can experiment with it and ultimately discern for ourselves what is helpful and what is not. By doing this, we can ensure that our traditions are still important and alive and learn more about the world around us.

4. Go within for Understanding

There are many ways to learn about and understand the world around us. One way is to look to the past and learn from the traditions of those who came before us. Another way is to go *within ourselves* for understanding. Each approach has its benefits and drawbacks, but both can be useful in different situations.

Looking to the past can give us a better understanding of where we come from and how we got to where we are today. It can help us see the interconnectedness of all things and how our actions have ripple effects extending far into the future. However, it can also be easy to get caught up in nostalgia or dwell on how things used to be "better." To truly learn from tradition, we must be willing to question why things are done the way they are and whether there might be a better way.

Going within ourselves for understanding can help us find our truth and develop our unique perspective on the world. It can also help us connect with our deepest desires and create a more authentic life. However, this approach can also be challenging because it requires us to step out of our comfort zones and face our fears. It can be easy to get lost in our thoughts and miss what is happening right in front of us. To truly learn from going within, we must be open to what we find there, even if it is uncomfortable or scary.

5. There Is No One Right Path

We can take many different paths in life, and each tradition has its own wisdom to offer. By learning from things that are different from our way, we can get a complete view of the world and find our own way. There is no one right path, but by studying other traditions, we can learn how to live more holistic and fulfilling lives. Each tradition has its way of looking at the world, and by exposure to multiple traditions, we can develop a more nuanced understanding of reality. By learning from different traditions, we can also learn to respect and value the different ways people have lived as we develop our own unique and authentic paths.

6. All Traditions Have Value

There are many ways to learn from traditions. One way is to observe and compare the similarities and differences between our traditions and those of others. By doing this, we can learn more about the value of all traditions and understand them better. Another way to learn from traditions is to take part in them ourselves. This can involve anything from attending religious ceremonies to participating in cultural festivals. Participating in the tradition gives us first-hand knowledge and experience of its meaning and purpose. No matter what method we use, learning from tradition is essential to developing our understanding of the world around us.

7. Respect the Beliefs of Others

Each year, billions of people worldwide celebrate religious and cultural holidays. Though these traditions may differ in many ways, they all share a common purpose: to bring people together. In an increasingly divided world, it is more necessary than ever to respect others' beliefs. One way to do this is to learn about the traditions that they hold dear. By learning about the history and meaning of holidays and traditions, we can better understand how rich our shared humanity is. In addition, we can learn about their values and perspectives when interacting with people from other cultures. Ultimately, embracing diversity can help us build a more compassionate and understanding world.

8. Be Open-Minded and Willing to Learn

One of the best things about traditions is that they can be passed down through generations, giving us a sense of connection to our past. But what if we're not connected to that tradition? Can we still learn from it? *Absolutely!* We can better understand other cultures and customs by being curious and willing to learn. Learning about other traditions can also help us appreciate our heritage. So next time you're presented with an unfamiliar tradition, don't be afraid to give it a try. You might just find that you have a lot to learn from it.

9. Take What Works for You and Leave the Rest

People follow many different traditions, whether it is a religion, culture, or way of life. While some traditions are very old and passed down for generations, others are fairly new and still evolving. Regardless of its age, each tradition has something to offer. The key is to take what works for you and leave the rest. For example, suppose you grew up in a family that always ate dinner together but now live independently. In that case, you might continue that tradition by making sure to sit down for a meal by yourself every night. Or, if you don't like how your workplace operates, you might take inspiration from another company's model and implement some of their practices in your business. Do not be afraid to experiment and find what works best for you. Tradition can be a great source of wisdom and knowledge, but remember that you don't have to follow it blindly. You can cherry-pick the parts that work for you and create your own unique tradition.

10. Have a Sense of Humor

No matter how serious, any tradition can be improved by a sense of humor. This may seem a strange sentiment to have at first since humor is usually seen as the opposite of seriousness and respect. And reverence. However, a healthy dose of humor can help us appreciate the things we hold dear. When we take ourselves too seriously, we can become rigid and inflexible, missing out on the joy that comes from laughter. A sense of humor also allows us to see the world from different perspectives and find common ground. Kabbalah has also influenced hermeticism and the Order of the Golden Dawn. Jewish mystics have long used a set of teachings to figure out what the Hebrew Bible means. Today, people from all walks of life can learn from and appreciate the wisdom of Kabbalah.

There is no single *right way* to learn about and understand the world around us. Most importantly, we are open to learning in whatever way works best for us at any given moment. Sometimes that means looking at the past, and sometimes it means looking within ourselves. The key is to remain open to all possibilities and never to stop learning.

Chapter 2: Can Anyone Become a Kabbalist?

For centuries, Kabbalah was known to be hidden or secret knowledge accessible only to selected individuals who met certain criteria. Initiates into this tradition had to study the Torah and other sacred texts, be male and be at least 40 years old. In recent years, however, these criteria have fallen away, and increasing numbers of rabbis and scholars are making Kabbalah accessible to the masses, regardless of gender, age, or background.

Rabbis and scholars are making Kabbalah accessible to the masses.
https://pixabay.com/es/photos/estrella-de-david-estrella-s%c3%admbolo-458372/

In this chapter, we will explore the changing landscape of Kabbalah and the key concepts that anyone can learn. We will also provide practical advice on how to study this ancient wisdom tradition.

The Changing Scenario of Kabbalah

Kabbalah, which is also called Jewish mysticism, is a group of ancient teachings about how to live a meaningful and happy life. Kabbalah has been passed down through the generations for centuries, providing insight into the nature of God, the universe, and the human soul. In recent years, however, there has been a growing interest in Kabbalah by people of all backgrounds and religious beliefs. This is partly because Kabbalah provides a unique perspective on some of life's most pressing questions, such as "What is the meaning of life?" and "How can I achieve happiness and fulfillment?"

As more and more people seek answers to these questions, Kabbalah is likely to continue to grow in popularity. The good news is that anyone can learn Kabbalah, regardless of age, gender, or religious affiliation. In the past, Kabbalah was passed down orally from teacher to student. Still, nowadays, there are many ways to learn this ancient wisdom tradition—online courses, books, and a plethora of websites.

Many people find that the best way to learn Kabbalah is to find a teacher or mentor who can guide them through the material. Others prefer to study independently, using books, online resources, and courses. Whichever method you choose, the most important thing is to have an open mind and a willingness to learn.

Kabbalah for All

One of the most common misconceptions about Kabbalah is that it is only for certain people, such as rabbis or scholars. Some of the most famous Kabbalists, such as Christian mystics like Meister Eckhart and Teresa of Avila, were not Jewish.

Kabbalah is open to everyone because it is *not a religion*. Rather, it is a *wisdom tradition* that people of any belief system can use. Kabbalah teaches us that there is one God, but this *one God* is not necessarily the same as the God of Judaism, Christianity, or Islam. Instead, Kabbalah teaches that God is a mysterious force humans cannot fully understand. This may sound strange, but it is very freeing.

It means you do not need to believe in a specific God to learn and benefit from Kabbalah.

The Criteria for Learning Kabbalah

So, if anyone can learn Kabbalah, what are the criteria for doing so? There are no hard and fast rules; however, a few things will help you understand Kabbalah more effectively. First of all, it is helpful to have some knowledge of Judaism or any other religious tradition. Armed with this kind of knowledge, you will not find the concepts of God and religious rituals strange and difficult to understand. However, it is not essential, and many resources are available to help you learn about Kabbalah.

Another helpful criterion for learning Kabbalah is a willingness to question every life lesson you think you've learned. Kabbalah is not about blindly accepting a set of beliefs. Instead, it is about constantly questioning and probing to gain a deeper understanding of the nature of reality. This can be challenging, but it is also incredibly rewarding!

Finally, it is also helpful to have some prior knowledge of meditation or other forms of introspective work. Kabbalah is very much about working on oneself, so it is helpful to have some experience in this area. However, once again, this is not essential. Many resources can teach you about meditation and other forms of inner work, even if you have no prior experience.

Key Concepts of Kabbalah

Kabbalah includes a system of ethical and spiritual practices designed to help people live in harmony with God and the natural world. Key concepts in Kabbalah include the Tree of Life, the Shekhinah, and Tikkun Olam. The Tree of Life is a symbol of the cosmic order, and it is used to represent the relationship between God and the universe. The Shekhinah is the feminine aspect of God, and Tikkun Olam is the Jewish concept of repairing the world. These concepts offer a way to understand the nature of reality and our place in it. They also guide how we can live our lives in a meaningful and fulfilling way.

1. Ein Sof

One of the key theories in Kabbalah is Ein Sof, which means "the infinite." This concept teaches that God is an infinite being who is beyond all human comprehension. Ein Sof is often represented as a circle with no beginning or end, symbolizing the infinite nature of God. Kabbalists believe that through the study and contemplation of Ein Sof, they can gain insights into the nature of reality and God's purpose for creation. The idea of Ein Sof is used to help people understand that the universe is not limited by what we can see and understand with our five senses. Instead, it is a vast and infinite reality beyond our full comprehension.

2. Sefirot

Sefirot (also spelled "sephiroth"), a series of 10 divine emanations representing different aspects of God, form the heart of Kabbalah. They are often depicted as a tree, with each successive level branching downward from the one above it. Together, they form the framework through which God creates and maintains the universe. The Sefiroth also provide a map for the soul's journey back to God. The Kabbalah belief is that the soul descends into the material world to gain experience and wisdom, and as the soul grows and matures, it begins to yearn for its spiritual source. The sefirot provide a path back to God; through them, the soul can be reunited with its divine source. Understanding and aligning oneself with the sefirot can deepen the connection to the Divine and achieve spiritual enlightenment.

3. Tzimtzum

Tzimtzum is another fundamental concept in Kabbalah. The word Tzimtzum means "contraction" or "withdrawal" and refers to the belief that God withdrew Himself from the world to allow creation to take place. This withdrawal allowed a space to open up in which the world could come into being. The concept of Tzimtzum is used to explain how the physical world came into existence and to describe God's relationship to the world. While Tzimtzum is a complex theological conception, it provides a helpful way of understanding some of the central mysteries of existence.

4. Shekhinah

The Shekhinah is the Divine Presence of God, which is said to dwell within all creation. In Kabbalistic thought, the Shekhinah is often seen as the feminine aspect of God and is sometimes referred to as the "Divine Mother." The Shekhinah is also seen as a powerful force for good, often invoked in prayers and rituals for protection and healing. While the concept of the Shekhinah may be complex, it is central to the Kabbalistic understanding of God and the Universe. The Shekhinah is a reminder that God is present in all things and that the Divine can be found in even the seemingly mundane aspects of life.

5. Tikkun Olam

Tikkun Olam is a Hebrew phrase that means "repair of the world." It is often used to refer to the idea of making the world a better place, and it is also a cornerstone belief t in the Jewish mystical tradition of Kabbalah. The ultimate goal of Tikkun Olam is to restore balance and harmony to the world, and Kabbalists believe this can be achieved through individual acts of kindness and compassion. Kabbalists also teach that we are all connected and that our actions have an impact on the entire world. As such, Tikkun Olam is about improving our lives and working together to create a better world for everyone.

6. The Messiah

In Kabbalah, the Messiah is *not seen* as a single person who will come to save the world. Instead, the Messiah is seen as an energy or force that will repair the world (Tikkun Olam). The coming of the Messiah is often seen as a metaphor for the process of spiritual enlightenment. In other words, the Messiah is not a person but an ideal that we can all strive to achieve. The actuality of the Messiah is central to Kabbalistic thought and provides a powerful way of understanding the ultimate goal of our lives.

7. The World to Come

The *World to Come* is a core tenet of Kabbalah. It refers to the belief that there is a time and place where all will be made right. The World to Come is often seen as a metaphor for heaven or the ultimate goal of our spiritual journey. In Kabbalah, it is believed that the world is constantly evolving and that each generation brings us closer to the World to Come. The concept of the World to Come is a reminder that our journey is not complete and that there is still more work to be done. With this in mind, we can strive to make the world better and bring ourselves closer to the divine.

8. Repentance

Repentance or atonement is another dominant tenet of Judaism and an important part of Kabbalah. Repentance means turning away from sin and returning to God. In Kabbalistic philosophy, it is seen as a powerful tool for spiritual growth. It is believed that we can purify our souls and become closer to God through repentance; it is also a way of asking for forgiveness. This essential part of the Jewish tradition provides a powerful way of understanding our relationship with God.

9. Free Will

Another essential part of the Jewish tradition, *free will* means that we have the power to choose our actions; we are not controlled by fate or destiny. In Kabbalistic thought, it is considered another powerful tool for spiritual growth; through its use, we can make choices that help us to become closer to God. It's also a way of taking responsibility for our own lives, providing a path to a better understanding of our relationship with God.

10. The Torah

The Torah is the central text of Kabbalah and contains a great deal of wisdom and knowledge. It is said that the Torah was revealed to Moses on Mount Sinai and that it contains the secrets of the universe. The Torah is divided into five books: Genesis, Exodus, Leviticus, Numbers, and Deuteronomy – and each book contains different laws and teachings. The Torah also includes the Ten Commandments, which are the basic principles of Kabbalah; understanding its contents is essential for understanding this mystical tradition.

How to Study Kabbalah

While it has been practiced for centuries by rabbis and other Jewish scholars, Kabbalah is not just for experts. The best way to learn Kabbalah is to find a reputable teacher or group to study with; as previously mentioned, many resources are available online and in libraries. Once you have found your best resource(s), read as much as possible about the topic. You may also want to attend workshops or classes taught by experienced practitioners. By immersing yourself in the material, you will gain a deeper understanding of its many important concepts.

Kabbalah can be a complex subject, but it is also incredibly rewarding. Here are some tips to help you get started:

1. Meditation

Kabbalah meditation is one of the main methods used to achieve this connection. During Kabbalah meditation, practitioners focus on a particular Hebrew letter or word. By repeating this letter or word, they focus their mind and open themselves up to divine guidance. As well as providing a deep sense of connection, this practice also helps to promote peace of mind, improve concentration, and reduce stress.

If you're interested in exploring this powerful form of meditation, you should know a few things before getting started. First, find a qualified teacher who can offer guidance and support. Secondly, be prepared for some challenging mental work - Kabbalah meditation is not for everyone. But if you're willing to put in the effort, this can be an incredibly rewarding experience.

2. Reading

Many Kabbalists believe that study is the key to unlocking the universe's secrets. While there are many different ways to study Kabbalah, one of the most essential is *reading*. By engaging with Kabbalistic texts, students begin to develop a deeper understanding of the mystical tradition. However, it is crucial to approach these writings with an open mind and a willingness to explore new ideas. It's not about acquiring knowledge; *it is about transformation.* As such, students should be prepared to question everything they think they know about the world and to view it in a new light. With time and effort, anyone can learn how to study Kabbalah. The journey begins with a simple act of reading.

3. Finding a Teacher

While the roots of Kabbalah date back thousands of years, it is a pearl of timeless wisdom relevant to people of all faiths and backgrounds. If you are interested in studying Kabbalah, consider finding a teacher who resonates with you and your spiritual journey. Many online resources and community groups can help guide you to a qualified teacher in your area. Once you have found him/her, commit to regular study and practice. Kabbalah is not simply a theoretical tradition; it is meant to be applied daily. By studying regularly and putting the principles of Kabbalah into practice, we can create more harmony and balance in our lives.

4. Practice

When we study Kabbalah, we are engaged in the process of self-discovery that can lead to greater clarity, confidence, and peace of mind. The practice of Kabbalah can help us to understand our relationships with others, our place in the world, and our spiritual nature. To get the most out of our studies, approach Kabbalah with an open mind, curiosity, and a willingness to experiment with new ideas. The following are some tips for getting the most out of your Kabbalah studies:

- **Read Widely:** There are many books available on Kabbalah, from introductory texts to more advanced treatises. By reading widely, you will gain a greater understanding of the different aspects of this complex tradition.

- **Study with a Group:** Studying Kabbalah with others can greatly deepen your understanding of the material and connect with like-minded individuals. If you don't have access to a formal study group, consider starting one yourself.

- **Practice What You Learn:** Learning about Kabbalah is only useful if you apply what you learn in your everyday life. Experiment with meditation and visualization techniques to see how they affect your thoughts, emotions, and behavior.

By following these tips, you can make the most out of your Kabbalah studies and reap the benefits of this ancient wisdom tradition.

5. Community

At its core are personal growth and spiritual evolution. Kabbalah teaches that we are all connected and that our actions impact others. Finding a community of like-minded individuals who can offer support and guidance is crucial, and again, online resources and local groups are your best bet. Find a teacher or guide who can offer personalized instruction and help you find your study path.

6. Service

A great way to Kabbalah is to offer service to others. When we give of ourselves without expectation of anything in return, we open our hearts and minds to new possibilities. We also come to understand that, as interconnected beings, our personal growth ultimately benefits the entire world. The following are some ways you can offer service to others:

- **Volunteer Your Time:** Many organizations could benefit from your time and energy. Consider volunteering at a local soup kitchen, Habitat for Humanity, or any other organization that speaks to you.

- **Donate Money:** If you are unable or unwilling to volunteer your time, consider making a financial contribution to a worthy cause.

- **Help a Friend:** Sometimes, the best way to help others is simply to be there for them. If you have a friend who is going through a tough time, offer your support. Listen to them, offer advice if asked, and just be a shoulder to cry on.

- **Be Kind:** One of the simplest and most effective ways to serve others is to simply be kind. Smile at strangers, hold the door open for someone, or just take the time to converse with someone. These small acts of kindness can make a big difference in the world.

By offering service to others, we make the world a better place and open ourselves up to new possibilities and experiences.

Kabbalah is an ancient wisdom tradition that offers a unique perspective on the nature of reality. It is a complex system of thought that can be difficult to understand, but the rewards of study are well worth the effort. Kabbalah can help us to understand our place in the world and to see the interconnectedness of all things. It also provides a framework for personal growth and spiritual evolution. Finding a community of like-minded individuals who can offer support and guidance is important to get the most out of your studies.

And finally, remember that one of the best ways to learn Kabbalah is to offer service to others. By following these tips, you can make the most out of your studies and reap the many benefits of this ancient wisdom tradition.

Chapter 3: One Tree, Seven Chakras, and Four Worlds

Kabbalah teaches us that there is a spiritual dimension to reality and that we can tap into this dimension to experience a more profound sense of meaning and purpose in our lives. Through the process of Kabbalah, we can learn to connect with this spiritual realm and use its power to create change in our lives; it provides a way to understand and work with the spiritual forces that are all around us.

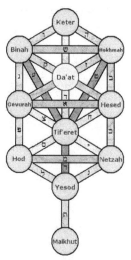

The Tree of Life is one of the foremost symbols in Kabbalah.
https://commons.wikimedia.org/wiki/File:Ktreewnames.png

The Tree of Life is a key principle in Kabbalah. This chapter will give an overview of the Tree of Life and how it is used to explain both the big and small picture. We will also examine the links between the Tree of Life, sacred geometry, and the Hindu and Buddhist traditions' seven main chakras. By understanding these concepts, we can begin to tap into the spiritual power of Kabbalah.

The Kabbalistic Tree of Life

The Tree of Life is one of the foremost symbols in Kabbalah, which is a Jewish mystical tradition. The tree is made up of 10 spheres, called *sephiroth*, each showing a different part of God. These spheres are connected by 22 paths, representing the soul's journey as it ascends to Godhood. The Tree of Life is a map of reality, and its sephiroth and courses offer a way to understand the divine nature of Creation. People also believe that a tree is a powerful tool for meditation and thinking. Visualizing the tree can teach you a lot about reality and your place in it.

The Tree of Life has been an important part of the Kabbalah for hundreds of years, and anyone who wants to learn from it can still do so. The tree can be used as a tool for meditation and contemplation. Traditionally, Kabbalists would sit with the tree in front of them and focus their attention on each individual sephirah. As they did so, they would meditate on the qualities of that sephirah and how they related to their own lives. In this way, the tree could be used as a tool for self-discovery and growth.

The Tree's Role in Describing the Macrocosm and the Microcosm

The tree is important because it can represent both the big (macro) and small (micro) picture; the macrocosm is the universe as a whole, and the microcosm is the individual human being. The tree can be seen as a map of reality, with each sephirah representing a different aspect of the universe. It can also be seen as a model of the human psyche, with each sephirah representing a different side of the self.

The tree is also significant because it shows the *relationship between* the macrocosm and the microcosm. Kabbalists use the Tree of Life (the sephirot diagram) to figure out what God is like and how the universe works. The tree is often shown as a person's body, with the head standing for God, the trunk for the world that God made, and the branches for the different levels of reality. The Tree of Life is an ancient symbol used by numerous cultures throughout history. The Tree of Life is a powerful symbol of life. It is often shown as a big tree with branches reaching up to the sky and roots deep into the ground.

In addition to being a map of reality, it is also an important way to explain how the big and small picture fit together. The branches represent the heavens, while the roots represent the underworld. The tree trunk, which connects the two, symbolizes the journey between these two realms. This journey is known as the "Middle Way," which is believed to be the key to achieving balance in one's life.

The Tree of Life is also often used to symbolize the human body. In this comparison, the tree's head stands for God, the trunk for the human body, and the branches for the different levels of reality. Just as the tree has roots that extend into the ground, so does the human body have roots (the feet) connecting it to the earth. And just as the tree has branches that reach up to the sky, so does the human body have branches (arms) extending out into the world.

Kabbalistic teaching says that the universe is a reflection of God and that each level of reality is like a different part of God. The Sephiroth, or spheres of the tree, symbolize these different aspects, and the paths connecting them represent the soul's journey as it ascends to Godhood. In other words, the Tree of Life is a map of reality, and its sephiroth and paths offer a way to understand the divine nature of Creation.

The tree is a powerful symbol of life, and its wisdom can be used to understand both the macrocosm and the microcosm. By understanding the tree, we can begin to understand the nature of reality and our place within it.

The Connections between the Tree and the Sacred Geometry

The *Tree of Life* is often used in conjunction with other symbols, such as the *Flower of Life* and the *Seed of Life*. These symbols are all based on sacred geometry, which is the study of the patterns found in nature. Sacred geometry is used to understand the relationship between the physical and spiritual worlds.

The Flower of Life is a symbol that consists of overlapping circles. It is said to represent the cycle of life, death, and rebirth.

The Seed of Life is a symbol that consists of seven overlapping circles. It is said to represent the seven days of creation, and it is often used in conjunction with the Tree of Life.

The Tree of Life and the Flower of Life are both based on the Fibonacci sequence. In the Fibonacci sequence, each number is the sum of the two numbers that came before it. The Fibonacci sequence begins with 0 and 1 and goes on to infinity. The relationship between the Tree of Life and the Fibonacci sequence is simple - each sephira on the Tree of Life corresponds to a number in the Fibonacci sequence.

The first sephira, Kether, corresponds to the number 0, while the second sephira, Chokmah, corresponds to the number 1. The third sephira, Binah, corresponds to the number 2, and so on. This relationship between the Tree of Life and the Fibonacci sequence is known as the "Fibonacci Code." The Fibonacci Code is a way of understanding the relationship between the physical and spiritual worlds. It is based on the idea that everything in the universe is connected - and there is a pattern to this connection.

The Tree of Life can be used to understand the Fibonacci Code. By understanding the symbolism of the Tree of Life, we can understand the patterns found in nature.

The Tree of Life and the Chakras

The Tree of Life is also often used in conjunction with the chakras. The chakras are energy centers in the human body that are said to be responsible for our physical, mental, and emotional health. There are seven main chakras, each associated with a different sephira on the Tree of Life.

The first chakra, the root chakra, is located at the base of the spine. It is associated with sephira Malkuth. The second chakra, the sacral chakra, is located in the lower abdomen. It is associated with the sephira Yesod. The third chakra, the solar plexus chakra, is located in the upper abdomen. It is associated with the sephira Hod.

The fourth chakra, the heart chakra, is found in the center of the chest. It is associated with the sephira Tiphereth. The fifth chakra, the throat chakra, is in the throat. It is associated with the sephira Netzach. The sixth chakra, known as the third eye chakra, is located in between the eyebrows. It is associated with the sephira Hod. The seventh chakra, the crown chakra, is at the top of the head. It is associated with the sephira Kether.

In Hinduism, the chakras are said to be responsible for our physical, mental, and emotional health. Buddhism also knows how important the chakras are, and people often use them when they meditate. The chakras can be used to understand the Tree of Life. By understanding the relationship between the chakras and the Tree of Life, we can understand the connection between the physical and spiritual worlds.

The Four Kabbalistic Worlds

There are four holistic worlds, each with its unique energy and purpose.

The **first world** is called Atzilut, and it is the world of *pure spirit*. It is the highest and most rarefied of the four worlds and is where God resides. Also known as the world of archetypes, this is the world of pure ideas, where everything is perfect and unified.

The **second world** is called Beriyah, the world of Creation. It is here that the physical universe comes into existence. This is the world of form, where things take shape and begin to interact with each other.

The **third world** is called Yetzirah, the world of formation. It is here that the energy of Creation takes form and substance. This is the world of action and reaction, where things come into being and interact with each other.

The **fourth and final world** is called Assiah, and it is the world of action. It is here that our thoughts and deeds take shape in the physical world. This is the world of manifestation, where things exist in time and space.

Each of these four worlds has an important role in spiritual development. To grow spiritually, we must first connect with the world of pure spirit (Atzilut). From there can begin to create our reality in the world of Creation (Briah). Once we have created our reality, we can begin to give it form and substance in the world of formation (Yetzirah). Finally, we can bring our thoughts and deeds into physical manifestation in the world of action (Assiah). The Tree of Life is a map that helps us understand the relationship between these four worlds. It is a useful tool for anyone who wants to learn more about life's mysteries.

1. Atziluth

Atziluth is the highest of the four worlds in Kabbalistic thought. It is the world of divine emanation, where God's light and love first flow forth. This is the realm of pure spirit, where all is unity, and there is no duality or division. From Atziluth comes the light that illuminates all the other worlds. In Jewish tradition, Atziluth is often called the World to Come because it is the source of all blessings and perfections. Those who dwell in Atziluth are said to be close to God, and they enjoy a state of perpetual bliss.

The name *Atziluth* comes from a Hebrew root that means "to go forth." This means that Atziluth is the world from which all others come. It is also sometimes called the World of Emanations because it is where divine energies first flow forth. In Kabbalah, ten sefirot, or divine emanations, represent different aspects of God's nature. These Sefirot begin in Atziluth and flow down into the other threads. Each sefirah has its own characteristic energy and color. Together, they all make up a reality map showing how everything in creation is interconnected, which is what the Tree of Life means. Everything originates from Atziluth and flows down through the other worlds before returning to its source.

Those who dwell in Atziluth are said to be close to God and enjoy a state of permanent bliss. This world is often described as a place of great light and beauty. In Kabbalistic writing, Atziluth is often compared to the material world, which is seen as a dark and distorted reflection of the real world. The things we see in this world are only shadows of their true counterparts in Atziluth. But even though our world isn't a perfect copy of Atziluth, there are still bits of divine light in it. By studying Kabbalah and meditating on the nature of reality, we can glimpse Atziluth and experience some of its peace and bliss in our lives.

---

2. Briah

The Kabbalistic world of Briah is a realm of pure thought and potential. It is the world of the divine architect, of unformed matter awaiting the shaping hand of God. In Briah, everything is possible, and nothing is concrete. It is a world of infinite potential and limitless possibility.

The Kabbalists teach that Briah is the world that we create through our thoughts and actions. Every thought and every deed brings into existence a new reality. This is why it is so important to be mindful of our thoughts and actions, for they have the power to shape our world. The Kabbalists also teach that we have the power to choose which reality we want to create. We can choose love or fear, harmony or discord, light or darkness. The choice is ours.

Briah is also the world of miracles. In Briah, all things are possible, and so miracles are commonplace. Miracles are not violations of natural law; they are simply manifestations of the unlimited power of God. If we open our hearts and minds to the possibility of miracles, they will surely come into our lives.

The Kabbalistic world of Briah is a realm of boundless potential and limitless possibility. It is a world that we create through our thoughts and actions. And it is a world where miracles are commonplace. What more could we ask for?

3. Yetzirah

Yetzirah is the third of the four Kabbalistic worlds, and it is sometimes referred to as the world of formation. In this world, the Divine light is clothed in various forms, giving rise to all of the manifold creaturely life that we see around us. While our physical world is Yetzirah's lowest manifestation, it is by no means the only one. The spiritual realms above us are also part of Yetzirah, and each has its unique form and character. Just as we ascend from the physical to the mental and spiritual realms, so can we descend from Yetzirah into the lower worlds. By doing so, we can gain a deeper understanding of the nature of reality and our place within it.

4. Assiah

In the Kabbalistic tradition, each world is a more spiritual level of reality, with Assiah being the most physical and Atzilut being the most spiritual. Even though we live in all four worlds every day, most of us don't know about the higher levels of reality that exist above the physical world. Kabbalists believe that it is our task in life to raise our consciousness to these higher levels to bring more spirituality into our lives and help create a better world. By gaining a better understanding of the Kabbalistic concept of Assiah, we can begin to see the world around us in a new light and open ourselves up to a deeper level of understanding.

Kabbalah is a mystical tradition that teaches about the nature of reality and our place within it. It is a system of thought that can help us understand the world and our place within it. Kabbalah can also help us connect with our higher selves and the Divine. Kabbalah is a tradition open to everyone, regardless of religious affiliation.

The Tree of Life is a central symbol in Kabbalah, and it can be used to understand the nature of reality and our place within it. The connection between the chakras and the Tree of Life helps us understand the relationship between our physical bodies and spiritual selves. The chakras are energy centers that run along the spine from the base to the crown. They are connected to the body's major organs and represent different aspects of our being, and each chakra is associated with a different level of reality. They can be used to understand the nature of reality and our place within it.

The Tree of Life is divided into four worlds, each representing a different level of reality. The Kabbalistic tradition teaches us that there are four levels of reality, each progressively more spiritual than the last. The physical world is Assiah, the world of action. The mental world is Yetzirah, the world of formation. The spiritual world is Briah, the world of creation, and the divine world is Atzilut, the world of emanation. Even though we live in all four worlds every day, most of us don't know about the higher levels of reality that exist above the physical world. Kabbalists believe that it is our task in life to raise our consciousness to these higher levels to bring more spirituality into our lives and help create a better world.

Chapter 4: The Sephirot I. The Supernal Triad

The Kabbalistic Tree of Life is composed of 10 spiritual principles or Sephirot. The first three sephiroth are called the supernal triad, symbolizing the highest level of spirituality a human can attain. The supernal triad comprises Kether, Chokmah, and Binah. In the previous chapter, we introduced the concept of the Kabbalistic tree of life and explained what a sephirah is.

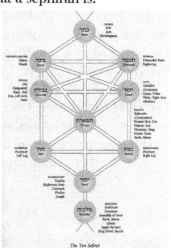

The first three sephiroth are called the supernal triad.
Edaina, CC BY-SA 3.0 <http://creativecommons.org/licenses/by-sa/3.0/>, via Wikimedia Commons: https://commons.wikimedia.org/wiki/File:The_one_tr%C3%A4d.jpg

The Sephirot are the 10 divine emanations of God, and each one corresponds to a different side of the human experience. In this chapter, we will focus on the first three sephirot, known as the Supernal Triad. These sephirot correspond to the highest level of reality, known as the world of Atziluth.

Kether is the first sephirah, and it symbolizes the divine principle. It is the highest level of spirituality that a human can attain. Chokmah is the second sephirah, and it symbolizes wisdom. Binah is the third sephirah, and it symbolizes understanding.

The supernal triad is often represented as a triangle, with Kether at the top, Chokmah in the middle, and Binah at the bottom. This is because the three sephirot are considered to be interrelated and mutually supportive. Each sephirah has its unique qualities, but they all work together to create a harmonious whole. In this chapter, we will explore the individual qualities of each sephirah in the supernal triad.

The Supernal Triad

The Supernal Triad is one of the key concepts in Kabbalah. This is the belief that there are three levels of reality: the physical world, the spiritual world, and the divine world. Each level has its laws and principles. The physical world is governed by the laws of physics; the spiritual world is governed by the laws of karma, and the divine world by the will of God. Kabbalists believe that we can access all three levels of reality through our thoughts, words, and actions. By aligning our lives with the highest level of reality, we create positive change in ourselves and the world around us.

The Supernal Triad comprises three sephirot: Kether, Binah, and Chokmah. Each of these sephirot corresponds to a different Pillar of Reality. The Pillar of Severity represents Kether, the first sephirah; the Pillar of Mercy represents Binah, the second sephirah; and the Pillar of Balance represents Chokmah, the third sephirah. The three Pillars of Reality are the foundation upon which all of existence is built. To understand the nature of reality, we must first understand the nature of these three Pillars.

Each sephirah in the Supernal Triad is composed of the other two sephirot. For example, Kether is composed of Binah and Chokmah, Binah is composed of Kether and Chokmah, and Chokmah is composed of Kether and Binah. This is because each sephirah contains the energy of the other two sephirot. The Supernal Triad is, therefore, a microcosm of the entire tree of life, the highest level of reality, and it contains all of the other sephirot within it.

The Structure of the Triad

The Supernal Triad is structured in a particular way. The first sephirah, Kether, is masculine; the second sephirah, Binah, is feminine; and the third sephirah, Chokmah, is balanced. This structure reflects the duality of existence. Kabbalah teaches that everything in the universe is composed of two opposing forces: male and female, light and dark, good and evil. This duality is necessary for existence. Without it, there would be no motion, change, or life.

The Supernal Triad also reflects the trinity of existence. Kabbalah teaches that there are three elements to every experience: mind, body, and spirit. Every thought, every feeling, and every action has a mental, physical, and spiritual component. This trinity is necessary for existence. Without it, we would not be able to understand or experience reality.

The Supernal Triad is the foundation of the Tree of Life. It is the blueprint for existence. Everything that exists in the universe is a reflection of the Supernal Triad. By understanding the nature of the Supernal Triad, we can begin to understand the nature of reality.

The supernal triad is considered to be the highest level of spirituality because it represents the purest form of divine energy. This is the level where we can commune with God directly, without the interference of the material world. When we reach this level, we will directly understand the divine principle.

The supernal triad also forms the base for all other sephirot. Just as a house cannot stand without a strong foundation, the other sephirot cannot exist without the support of the supernal triad. If you are interested in reaching the supernal triad, it is crucial to understand the nature of each sephirah. In the next section, we will look closely at each sephirah in the supernal triad and explore its unique qualities.

Kether - The Pillar of Severity

Kether is the first Sephiroth on the Tree of Life, representing pure Spirit. It is considered the highest point on the Tree, and the crown symbolizes it. In some treatments, Kether is also known as the Ain Soph or the limitless light. Echoing this idea of limitlessness, Kether is often said to be both formless and devoid of any qualities. It might be tough to comprehend at first, but remember that Kether is also the origin of all Manifestations. Everything that exists stems from Kether, which means it contains the potential for everything. Even though it may seem formless and without qualities, Kether is still the source of all Creation - an important distinction to remember.

Relation to Divinity

Kether is the closest sephirah to the divine realm. It is said to be the first spark of creation and contains the potential for all other sephirot. Kabbalists believe that we can access the divine realm through Kether. By meditating on Kether, we can connect with the highest level of reality and tap into God's infinite wisdom and power.

Kether, also known as the Crown, sits at the top of the tree, above all the other sephirah, representing unity and pure divine energy. Every sephira is a part of Kether and is present in all things. Kether is often seen as a symbol of God or the Divine Mind. It is infinite and unchanging, and it represents our highest potential. We all aspire to reach the level of unity and wholeness that Kether represents. When we do, we will find that we are truly connected to the Divine.

Exercise

There are many ways to connect with Kether. One is to meditate on the sephirah. Sit in a comfortable position and close your eyes. Visualize a bright, white light above you. See this light growing larger and brighter until it surrounds you. This is the energy of Kether. Feel the energy of Kether flowing through you. Experience the unity and wholeness that it represents. Allow yourself to be filled with the light of Kether.

Another exercise is to think about a time when you felt connected to something greater than yourself. It could be a religious or spiritual experience or simply a moment when you felt a deep sense of peace and connection. What did that experience feel like? How did it change your perspective on life? Spend some time writing about that experience and what it meant to you. Then, reflect on how you can bring that feeling into your everyday life. What small steps can you take to help you feel more connected to the Divine?

Binah - The Pillar of Mercy

Binah is the second sephirah on the Tree of Life and represents understanding. The yin-yang symbol symbolizes it and is often referred to as the Great Mother. Binah is considered to be the feminine aspect of God and is said to be the source of all manifestation. It is her role to bring forth life from the womb of potentiality. In the same way, Binah is responsible for giving birth to our ideas and plans. She is the archetype of the great Cosmic Mother who brings new life into existence. Binah is often seen as a symbol of wisdom; we can understand the world around us through Binah. Without Binah, there would be no creation.

Binah is also known as the Pillar of Mercy because she is the one who bestows compassion and pardon upon us. She helps us to see the good in others, even when they have done wrong. Binah teaches us to forgive and reminds us that we are all connected in the web of life. When we show mercy to others, we are showing mercy to ourselves. Binah is the realm of pure love; we can receive divine guidance and wisdom through her grace.

Masculine and Feminine Aspects

In the Kabbalistic tradition, Binah is often represented by the color black; her symbol is the yin-yang. Binah is the mother of all the other sephirot and is seen as the embodiment of compassion and wisdom. Her chief characteristic is mercy. Binah also has a masculine aspect known as Chokhmah. Chokhmah is associated with the color white, and his symbol is the sun. Chokhmah is considered to be the father of all the sephirot, and he represents willpower and intelligence. He is also known for his justice and can be very stern when necessary. Together, these two aspects of Binah help to create a balanced universe.

Relation to Chokmah

Binah is traditionally seen as being in a relationship of receptivity to Chokmah, the second sephira, and the Masculine Divine. In other words, Binah receives creative energy from Chokmah and gives birth to manifestation. Binah is also seen as the Great Mother, giving form to Chokmah's energy through her womb. She is often seen as a dark or shadowy figure because she is also associated with the Underground World, where new life is formed. Binah is a powerful and necessary part of Creation, without which manifestation would not be possible.

Exercise

Meditating on Binah can help us to connect with our feminine energy and wisdom. It can also help us understand receptivity's role in manifestation. Spend some time in meditation, visualizing yourself as Binah. Allow yourself to receive the creative energy of the Universe and give birth to your deepest desires. Ask Binah to show you the way to compassion and wisdom, and allow her to fill you with her love and mercy.

When you are ready, close your eyes and begin to breathe deeply. Allow your mind to become still and focused. Imagine a column of white light descending from the heavens and entering through the top of your head. This is the light of Chokmah, the father principle. Feel this light enter your being and fill you with its radiant energy. Now imagine a column of black light rising from the earth and entering through the bottom of your feet. This is the light of Binah, the mother principle. Feel this light enter your being and fill you with its loving energy.

Allow these two lights to meet in the middle of your body, and feel their energies merge. You begin to feel a sense of balance and harmony as they merge. Allow yourself to be filled with the light of Binah and Chokmah. Feel their love and wisdom enter your being. Allow yourself to receive their guidance and direction. When you are ready, open your eyes and allow yourself to return to the present moment.

Take some time to journal about your experience. What did you see? What did you feel? What guidance did Binah and Chokmah offer you? Allow their wisdom to guide you in your life from this day forward.

Chokmah - The Pillar of Balance

Chokmah, the second sephirah, is known as the pillar of balance. It represents the masculine principle of creation and is associated with the element of air. The goal of Chokmah is to achieve a balance between the extremes of form and formlessness. This is symbolized by the image of a scale, with one side representing form and the other side representing formlessness. To achieve balance, Chokmah must find the middle between these two extremes. By doing so, it helps to bring harmony to the universe.

Chokmah is considered to be the first sephirah because it is the source of all creative energy. Chokmah is associated with the color white, and its symbol is the sun. The sun is seen as a symbol of life-giving energy, representing the power of Chokmah to create and sustain life.

Chokmah is a powerful sephirah, and all of the other sephirot feel its energy. It is the source of all creative power, and it is from this power that manifestation occurs. Chokmah is also associated with wisdom. Wisdom is the ability to see things from a higher perspective and understand reality's true nature. It is the knowledge that comes from understanding the relationships between all things.

Wisdom is a necessary part of the balance; it is through it that Chokmah brings harmony to the universe. By understanding the true nature of reality, Chokmah can see the relationships between all things. This understanding allows Chokmah to find the middle way between the extremes of form and formlessness. In this way, Chokmah brings balance to the universe.

Relation to Binah and Kether

Chokmah, the second sephira on the Tree of Life, is considered to be the "Father" principle. It is associated with the element of air and the colors white and silver. Chokmah is positioned opposite Binah on the Tree, and together they form the "Supernal Triangle." Above them is Kether, the first sephira. While Chokmah is considered very active and dynamic, Binah is more passive and receptive.

Together, these three sephirot represent the beginning of Creation. Kether is the point of origin, while Chokmah and Binah represent the first two stages of manifestation. In some ways, they can be thought of as the "Big Bang," followed by the universe's expansion. Together, these three sephirot embody the creative power of God.

Active Imagination Exercise

One way to connect with the energy of Chokmah is through active imagination. This is a process where you use your imagination to connect with the divine. To begin, find a quiet place where you will not be disturbed. Close your eyes and take several deep breaths. Then, allow your mind to wander. Visualize yourself walking through a beautiful garden. Notice the colors, smells, and textures around you.

As you explore, you come across a door. Open the door and step into a new world. What do you see? Spend some time exploring this new place. When you are ready, return to the present moment and take a few minutes to journal about your experience. An active imagination is a powerful tool for connecting with the sephirah of Chokmah. You can access hidden wisdom and bring creative ideas to life by exploring your inner world.

Da'at - The Hidden Sephirah

In the Kabbalistic tradition, there is a concept known as Da'at, which refers to hidden knowledge or wisdom. This hidden sephirah is said to be located at the center of the Tree of Life and is thought to be the source of all understanding. While the other sephirah can be studied and understood through traditional methods, Da'at is said to be beyond such means. It can only be accessed through direct experience, and this direct knowledge is said to lead to true enlightenment. In many ways, Da'at represents the ultimate goal of the Kabbalistic journey. It is where all understanding comes together, and it is from here that we can see the entire Tree of Life in its true form.

Connection to the Other Sephirot

Da'at is the final of the ten sephirot on the Kabbalistic Tree of Life, and it is thought to represent knowledge or understanding. Da'at is often depicted as a point of connection between the other sephirot and is seen as the place where all the different energies come together. In some ways, Da'at can be seen as the ultimate goal of the Tree of Life, representing a state of harmony and balance between all the different parts of the self. To reach Da'at, one must first go through a process of coming to know and understand oneself and then learn to see the same truths in others. Only when we have developed a deep connection to the other sephirot can we hope to attain Da'at.

Meditation Exercise

One way to connect with the energy of Da'at is through meditation. This is a process of quieting the mind and opening up to the flow of universal knowledge. To begin, find a comfortable place to sit or lie down. Close your eyes and take several deep breaths. Then, allow your mind to become still. Simply observe the thoughts and sensations that pass through your consciousness. Do not judge or analyze what you experience; simply let it be.

After a while, you may find that you enter into a state of deep peace and understanding. This is the energy of Da'at, and it is from here that true wisdom arises. Spend some time exploring this state of consciousness. When you are ready, return to the present moment and take a few minutes to journal about your experience. Meditation is a powerful tool for connecting with the sephirah of Da'at. By quieting the mind, you can access the hidden wisdom of the universe and bring greater understanding into your life.

The sephirot are best understood as a map of consciousness that can be used to navigate the inner landscape of the psyche. Each sephirah represents a different aspect of the self. By exploring these different energies, we can better understand who we are and what we are capable of. The sephirot can also be used as a tool for personal transformation. By working with the different energies represented by the sephirah, we can learn to create balance and harmony within ourselves and, in turn, bring more peace and happiness into our lives.

This chapter has introduced the concept of the sephirot and explored the first three sephiroth of the Tree of Life. In the next chapters, we will continue our journey down the Tree of Life and explore the remaining seven sephiroth. We will also learn about the mystical practice of Kabbalah and how it can be used to bring greater understanding and insight into our lives.

Chapter 5: The Sephirot II: The Ethical Triad

In the last chapter, we began to explore the symbolism of the sephirot - or the 10 divine emanations of God. We started with the top three sephirot on the Tree of Life, which belong to the world of Atzilut: Keter, Chokhmah, and Binah. In this chapter, we will move lower on the Tree of Life and explore the next trifecta of sephirot, which belongs to the world of Briah: Gevurah, Chesed, and Tiferet.

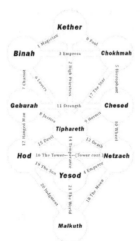

The three sephirot of the ethical triad are Gevurah, Chesed, and Tiferet.
Alan SyncBookPress, CC BY-SA 3.0 <https://creativecommons.org/licenses/by-sa/3.0>, via Wikimedia Commons: https://commons.wikimedia.org/wiki/File:Tree_of_Life_Tarot.jpg

This next group of sephirot is often called the "ethical triad" because they represent the three most important parts of ethical behavior: power, love, and beauty. Just as the previous sephirot represented different aspects of God, these sephirot also represented different aspects of the human soul. We will explore each sephirah in turn and see how we can use the symbolism of these divine emanations to help us lead more balanced and fulfilling lives.

The Ethical Triad

The three sephirot of the ethical triad are Gevurah, Chesed, and Tiferet. Gevurah is associated with power, Chesed with love, and Tiferet with beauty. These sephirot are arranged in a particular order on the Tree of Life. Gevurah is on the left, Chesed is on the right, and Tiferet is in the middle. This arrangement is significant because it shows the relationship between these sephirot. Gevurah and Chesed are opposite, just as power and love are opposite forces. Tiferet is in the middle because it is the synthesis of these two opposites. The balance between power and love is the essence of beauty.

This triad of sephirot also represents the three fundamental aspects of ethical behavior. Gevurah represents the ability to restrain oneself, Chesed represents the ability to give, and Tiferet represents the ability to find a middle way between these two extremes. These three sephirot teach us that the key to ethical behavior is balance. We must learn to restrain our power, so it does not become destructive, and we must learn to give of ourselves without becoming self-sacrificial. Only when we find this balance will we be able to act beautifully and ethically.

This triad is a three-part framework that can be used to evaluate ethical systems. It consists of three components: deontology, consequentialism, and virtue ethics. Deontology is the view that ethics is about duty and principle and that the right thing to do is determined by considering one's obligations. Consequentialism, on the other hand, is the view that the right thing to do is determined by considering the consequences of one's actions. Virtue ethics, finally, is the view that ethics is about developing character traits that enable one to live a good life.

Each of these points of view has its pros and cons, but they can be put together to make a stronger moral system. The Sephirot guides you towards a helpful way of thinking about these different ethics and how they relate to each other. These spheres belong to the Kabbalistic world of Briah. Gevurah is the masculine sephirah, Chesed is the feminine sephirah, and Tiferet is the child of these two opposites. In the following section, we will explore each sephirah in turn and see how they can help us create a more balanced and ethical life.

Gevurah: Power

The ethical triad comprises three sephirot, which are different aspects of God. The first, Gevurah, represents power. This sephirah is often linked to strictness and judgment because it shows the ability to set limits and control yourself. Gevurah is the quality of strength or severity. It is the ability to restrain oneself, to hold back, and be disciplined.

This sephirah is necessary for us to live a balanced and ethical life. Without Gevurah, we would be prone to excess and indulgence. We would have no self-control and no ability to set boundaries. We would be like children, acting on our instincts without any thought to the consequences of our actions. But Gevurah is not just about self-control. It is also about using our power wisely. This sephirah teaches us that we must use our power for good, not for evil. We must use our power to help others, not to harm them. And we must use our power to create, not to destroy.

Masculine Principle

In Jewish mysticism, Gevurah is the masculine principle, representing strength, discipline, and judgment. It is often compared to the Greek god Ares or the Roman god Mars. In the Kabbalah, Gevurah is associated with the fifth sefira, called Din or Judgment. It is also known as the "Left Hand of God." The feminine principle, Binah or Understanding, is represented by the right hand of God. Together, these two sefirot represent balance and harmony. While Gevurah represents the power to destroy, Binah represents the power to create. Without both of these forces, the universe would be in chaos.

The Force of Limitation

In the Jewish mystical tradition, Gevurah is the principle of judgment and limitation. It is the power that sets boundaries and

---

establishes order. Without Gevurah, the world would be in chaos. This force is symbolized by the color black, and it is associated with the element of fire. When we work with Gevurah energy, we align ourselves with the divine will and learn to trust in a higher power. We are also working to cultivate strength and discipline. By learning to control our energy, we can create meaningful change in our lives and the world around us.

The Power to Discern Good and Evil

In the Hebrew faith, Gevurah is the fifth sephirah or divine attribute. It is associated with justice, discipline, and the power to discern good from evil. Gevurah is often represented by a sword, which indicates its power to cut through lies and illusions. The followers of this faith believe that all have the power to discern right from wrong but that this power must be used wisely. We must learn to control our energy and use it for good, not evil. When we are faced with a difficult decision, it is through Gevurah that we can clearly see what is right and what is wrong. In this way, Gevurah helps us to maintain our integrity and live lives of honesty and truth.

The Quality of Justice

Gevurah is most often translated as "severity" or "strength," but it can also mean "justice." Justice is not always easy. It requires us to stand up for what is right, even when it is difficult or unpopular. It means being fair and unbiased and treating others with respect. Gevurah reminds us that justice is an essential aspect of a healthy society. Justice is not always easy, but it is always worth striving for. Gevurah reminds us of the importance of pursuing justice, even when it is hard. By doing so, we create a fairer world and justice for all.

Unlocking the Power of Gevurah

There are many ways to unlock the power of Gevurah in your life. One is to learn to control your energy. You can do this through practices like meditation, yoga, and breathwork. By learning to control your energy, you will become more aware of the energy around you and how it affects you. You will also be better able to use your energy for good.

Working on getting stronger and more disciplined is another way to open up the power of Gevurah. Martial arts, weightlifting, or any other activity that requires focus and discipline are excellent practices to awaken your power. By working on these things, you will develop the strength and discipline you need to stand up for what is right and to make meaningful changes in your life.

Lastly, you can also use Gevurah's power by learning about the teachings of the Hebrew faith. By understanding the principles of this faith, you will be better able to see what is right and wrong. You will also be better equipped to live a life of honesty and truth.

Chesed - The Power of Love

Chesed is the sphere of mercy in the ethical triad. It is associated with the element of water and the color blue. Chesed is the force that binds us together and allows us to feel compassion for others. It is through Chesed that we can give and receive love. In the Jewish mystical tradition, Chesed is the principle of love and compassion. The power brings us together and allows us to feel empathy for others.

Without Chesed, the world would be a cold and lonely place. When we work with Chesed energy, we are opening our hearts to love and compassion. We are also working to cultivate kindness and generosity. We can create a more loving and compassionate world by learning to give and receive love.

Feminine Principle

According to Jewish tradition, Chesed, which means "loving-kindness," is the highest and most important way to give. It is often linked to the feminine principle because it has qualities like mercy, compassion, and grace. Chesed is not simply a matter of performing acts of charity; rather, it is a way of being that stems from a deep inner wellspring of love and compassion. When we act from a place of Chesed, we do so without expectations or ulterior motives; we give simply because it is in our nature to do so. We may not always be aware of it, but every act of Chesed has the power to change our lives and the world around us for the better.

The Force of Expansion

In Judaism, the concept of Chesed is often translated as "loving-kindness." However, Chesed encompasses a much broader range of meanings than simply an act of kindness. The rabbis say Chesed helps us see beyond our own points of view and reach a place where we can understand and care about others.

In the Talmud, it is written that "the whole world is sustained by the merit of Chesed." This teaches us that acts of kindness are not only consequential in terms of our relationships, but they also have the power to positively impact the world at large. When we expand our loving-kindness to include all beings, we help create a more harmonious and whole world.

The Power of Love and Compassion

The Hebrew word Chesed also includes the ideas of compassion, goodwill, and loyalty, and it is often described as an act of mercy. It lies at the heart of many religious traditions. In the Jewish faith, the Talmud teaches us that Chesed should be extended not only to fellow Jews but to all human beings, regardless of race or religion.

Chesed also forms the basis for many acts of charity and altruism. By definition, it requires putting others before ourselves and acting with their best interests at heart. In a world that can sometimes seem driven by selfishness and greed, Chesed reminds us of the importance of love and compassion. Ultimately, Chesed is about creating a more just and caring world for all.

The Quality of Mercy

Chesed is often associated with compassion, love, and giving, representing how we express our love for others. It is the foundation of all human relationships and allows us to see the good in others even when they make mistakes. Chesed reminds us that everyone deserves to be treated with respect and understanding, and it gives us the strength to forgive. Chesed is not simply an emotion; it is an active choice to be loyal and faithful, even when it is difficult. It is a decision to show mercy, even when we do not feel like it. As we learn to show mercy towards others, we open ourselves up to receiving God's infinite mercy. In turn, this helps us to create a more compassionate world.

Unlocking the Power of Chesed

Chesed is a way of being that requires us to put others before ourselves and act with their best interests at heart. It is a quality of mercy and compassion that can improve our lives and the world around us. When we choose to extend Chesed to all beings, we help to create a more harmonious and whole world, and it is not simply an act of charity or goodwill.

There are many ways to show it in our daily lives. We can offer a kind word to someone who is having a tough day, help a neighbor with their groceries, or simply listen with an open heart. Every act of Chesed has the power to make a difference. We can help build a more just and loving world by choosing to be compassionate and merciful.

Tiferet - The Power of Beauty

Tiferet, often translated as "beauty," is the last of the three ethical sephirot. However, Tiferet encompasses a much broader range of meanings, including truth, balance, and harmony. In the Jewish tradition, Tiferet is often seen as the embodiment of compassion and mercy. The quality allows us to see the beauty in all things, even when they are difficult or painful. Tiferet is about finding balance amid chaos and harmony amid discord. It is a reminder that there is always hope for a better tomorrow – even in the darkest times.

The Child of Gevurah and Chesed

The sixth sephirah on the Kabbalistic Tree of Life, Tiferet, is the child of Gevurah and Chesed and embodies both of these qualities. On the one hand, Tiferet represents strength and discipline, while on the other hand, it represents compassion and mercy. This duality is what makes Tiferet such a powerful sephirah.

Tiferet teaches us that we must strike a balance between different aspects of our lives. We must be strong enough to face our challenges head-on, but we must also be compassionate enough to show mercy when needed. We hope to find true fulfillment in life by achieving this balance.

The Force of Balance

At the center of the Kabbalistic Tree of Life is the sefirah of Tiferet. This sephirah is often seen as a sign of balance because it brings together mercy and judgment, which are usually at odds with each other. Tiferet also represents the ideal human state, in which all our emotions and desires are in harmony. To achieve this balance, we must first move through a process of self-discovery, in which we come to understand our strengths and weaknesses. Only then can we learn to accept both our light and shadow sides and find the middle path that leads to wholeness. The sephirah of Tiferet reminds us that true balance comes from within, and it is only by understanding ourselves that we can hope to achieve it.

The Power of Beauty and Harmony

On a personal level, Tiferet represents our inner beauty and our ability to show that beauty to the world. When we are in touch with our own Tiferet, we can see the beauty in others and create relationships of mutual respect and admiration. We are also able to find meaning and purpose in our lives, even in the midst of difficult challenges. The power of Tiferet lies in its ability to transform our lives from the inside out, infusing them with beauty, balance, and harmony.

The Quality of Compassion

Tiferet is often represented as a rose, as it is seen as the link between opposites such as pleasure and pain, light and dark, and love and jealousy. Tiferet occupies a central position between Binah (understanding) and Chesed (loving-kindness) in the sephirot system. This placement reflects the belief that Tiferet represents the ideal balance between these two extremes. Tiferet also encompasses all the other sefirot, which makes it a powerful symbol of compassion. After all, what could be more compassionate than accepting all aspects of reality, both the light and the dark?

Unlocking the Power of Tiferet

Tiferet is a powerful sephirah that can help us to find balance and harmony in our lives. To unlock its power, we must first learn to accept all aspects of ourselves, both the light and the shadow. Once we have done this, we can begin to see the beauty in others and find compassion for them. We can also use Tiferet's power to give our lives meaning and direction. By lining up with the sephirah of Tiferet, we can try to reach a state of balance and harmony that will make our lives more enjoyable.

One way to begin working with Tiferet is to meditate on the qualities of balance and harmony. Visualize yourself surrounded by these qualities and feel them infusing your body and mind. Allow yourself to be filled with a sense of calm and well-being. As you meditate, repeat the following mantra:

"I am in touch with my inner beauty. I am surrounded by balance and harmony. I am filled with compassion for myself and others. I am

open to the possibilities of a more fulfilling life."

Another way to work with Tiferet is to focus on the quality of compassion. Visualize yourself surrounded by compassion, both for yourself and others. Allow yourself to feel the power of this quality infusing your body and mind. As you meditate, repeat the following mantra:

"I am surrounded by compassion. I am open to feeling the pain of others. I am willing to see the beauty in all things. I am committed to creating a more compassionate world."

As you work with Tiferet, remember that the goal is not to achieve perfection but to find balance and harmony in your life. Allow yourself to be imperfect, and know that this is part of the human experience. Embrace all aspects of yourself, both the light and shadow. By doing so, you will be well on your way to aligning with the sephirah of Tiferet.

The three ethical principles of Gevurah, Chesed, and Tiferet show the balance between different parts of reality. By aligning putting ourselves with these sephirot, we can strive to make our lives more balanced and harmonious. Through meditation and self-reflection, we can begin to work with these sephirot and unlock their power, and we'll create a more fulfilling life for ourselves and others. The key is to remember that the goal is not perfection but rather balance. So, embrace all aspects of yourself, both the light and the shadow. In doing so, you will be well on your way to achieving a more fulfilling life.

Chapter 6: The Sephirot III. From the Physical to the Astral

In the Kabbalistic tradition, Yetzirah is the second of the four worlds. This is the world of formation, where creative energy takes shape. The sephirot of Hod, Netzach, and Yesod are associated with this world. Hod represents rational thought and analysis, while Netzach stands for emotion and feeling. Yesod is the principle of change and transformation. It connects the other sephirot to the physical world. Yetzirah is a realm of potential and possibility where anything can be created. It is a place of imagination and creativity where we can bring our dreams and visions into reality.

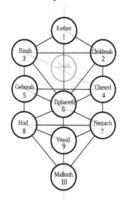

The sephirot of Hod, Netzach, and Yesod are associated with this world.
Cronholm144, CC BY-SA 2.5 <https://creativecommons.org/licenses/by-sa/2.5>, via Wikimedia Commons: https://commons.wikimedia.org/wiki/File:Tree_of_life_wk_02.svg

By working with the sephirot of Hod, Netzach, and Yesod, we can tap into our creative power and create the life we want to live. In this chapter, we will explore each of these sephirot and learn how to work with them to create the life we desire. We can start to move up to the higher realm of Assiah, the world of manifestation, by using the sephirot of Yetzirah.

The Last Triad

The Tree of Life is a mysterious symbol found in many different cultures and religions. For the Kabbalists, it represents the path to enlightenment and spiritual rebirth. The Tree is divided into ten sephiroth, or spheres, each representing a different aspect of God. The last triad, Hod, Netzach, and Yesod, represents the Tikkun Olam, or "repair of the world." These three sephiroth represent the principles of right action, right thought, and right speech. Together, they help us to create a more just and harmonious world. The Trees of Life can be found in many places, from ancient Egyptian temples to modern Jewish homes. They remind us that we are all connected and that we each have a role to play in making the world a better place.

While the sephirot of Hod, Netzach, and Yesod represent the higher realms of Yetzirah, the sephirah of Malchut represents the physical plane. Malchut is the principle of manifestation; through this sephirah, we can bring our dreams and visions into reality. By working with the sephirot of Yetzirah, we can start to rise to the higher realm of Assiah, the world of manifestation.

Hod - The Splendor of God

Hod is the eighth sephirah and is associated with glory and splendor. In the Bible, Hod is often used to describe the radiance of God's presence, as in the passage from Exodus: "And Moses went into the cloud, and ascended into Mount Sinai...And the Lord descended in the cloud, and stood with him there, and proclaimed the name of the Lord."

Hod is also associated with the left-hand path, which is sometimes seen as a path of excess and indulgence. However, Hod also represents balance and harmonious relationships. In Kabbalah, Hod is often paired with Netzach, the sephirah of victory, which helps to bring power and form to Hod's visionary creativity. Together, these two sephiroth offer a complete picture of divine revelation.

Hod is connected to the element of fire and stands for the idea of doing the right thing. It is the sephirah of righteous speech, and through it, we can express our truth. When we align our words with our highest and deepest truth, we can create miracles in our lives. We can also use the power of Hod to bring our dreams and visions into reality. The sephirah of Hod is also associated with the planet Mercury and is said to rule over the sign of Gemini. Gemini is known for its dual nature, reflected in the two faces of Hod: the face of glory and the face of excess.

The path to Hod begins with the sephirah of Chesed, and it is through this sephirah that we can access our divine nature. From Chesed, we move to Geburah, and through this sephirah, we can begin to purify our thoughts and deeds. As we move through the sephiroth, we reach Tiferet, the sephirah of balance and harmony. From Tiferet, we move to Netzach, the sephirah of victory, and through this sephirah, we can begin to manifest our dreams and visions. Finally, we reach Hod, the sephirah of right action, and it is through this sephirah that we can bring our truth into the world.

Symbolism

Hod Sephirah is one of the nine sephirot of the Kabbalistic Tree of Life. It is right in the middle of the tree, below Tiferet and above Netzach. Hod corresponds to the eighth day of Creation when God said, "Let there be light." In Jewish tradition, Hod is associated with splendor, glory, and majesty. The name Hod comes from the Hebrew word meaning "splendor" or "majesty." The sephirah is also associated with the element of earth.

Hod Sephirah represents the human need for balance and harmony. It is often thought of as a place of stillness and stability amid change and flux. Hod Sephirah is a symbol for the act of receiving, which we need to do to get blessings from above. When we are receptive, we are open to change and growth. We can also think of Hod Sephirah as a place of focus where we can direct our attention and energy to manifest our desires into reality.

Unlocking Hod

Kabbalistic tradition says that the Sephirah of Hod can be opened by being kind and humble. By doing nice things for other people, we make room in our hearts and minds for all the possibilities in the universe. As we let go of our ego-driven desires, we begin to tap into a higher source of wisdom and strength.

The Sephirah of Hod is also linked to the element of water, which stands for cleanliness and movement. To open Hod, we have to be ready to let go of our attachments and let the flow of universal energy guide us. When we do things that are for the best of all, we open the door to receiving an endless supply of good things.

There are many ways to unlock the power of Hod Sephirah. One way is to meditate on the sephirah's symbol, the two-faced lion. The lion represents strength, courage, and power. As we meditate on the lion, we can visualize ourselves as powerful creators capable of manifesting our dreams into reality. We can also use the power of Hod to purify our thoughts and deeds. By aligning our actions with our highest truth, we can create miracles in our lives.

Netzach-The Victory

Netzach, which means "victory" in Hebrew, is the seventh of the 10 sephirot in the Kabbalistic Tree of Life. It is associated with the element of fire and the planet Venus. Netzach is a strong sephirah showing how good wins over evil and light over darkness. It is a symbol of hope and strength in the face of adversity.

The path to Netzach begins with the sephirah of Chesed, and it is through this sephirah that we can access our divine nature. From Chesed, we move to Geburah, where we can begin to purify our thoughts and deeds. As we move through the sephiroth, we reach Tiferet, the sephirah of balance and harmony. From Tiferet, we move to Netzach, the sephirah of victory.

It is through Netzach that we can begin to manifest our dreams and visions. This sephirah is about the power of positive thinking and the ability to overcome any obstacle. When we align our thoughts and actions with our highest truth, we can create anything we desire. The key to using Netzach's power is to believe in our ability to make things happen.

When we tap into the energy of Netzach, we align ourselves with the forces of love and justice. We open ourselves up to limitless possibilities and potential. We become warriors for truth and compassion. We can see beyond our limitations and connect with something much greater than ourselves. In short, Netzach is the sephirah of transformation. It is the spark that ignites our journey toward wholeness and enlightenment.

Symbolism

The Netzach Sephirah is often symbolized by a rose representing balance and beauty. The rose is also a symbol of the Divine Feminine, and Netzach is often seen as the Sphere of Venus. It is associated with qualities such as love, compassion, and creativity.

In the Tree of Life, Netzach is found at the bottom of the left-hand column, opposite Hod. This placement symbolizes the fact that Netzach is receptive to energy, while Hod is an active one. Together, these two Sephiroth represent the perfect balance of masculine and feminine energy. Just as a rose has both thorns and petals, so does Netzach contain light and darkness. But when these opposites are in harmony, they create something truly beautiful.

The color associated with Netzach is green, representing growth, fertility, and new beginnings. Green is the color of springtime when the world comes alive after a long winter. It is the color of hope and possibility. When we work with the energy of Netzach, we open ourselves up to new possibilities and potential. We allow ourselves to grow and expand in all directions.

In the Tarot, Netzach is represented by the suit of cups. Water, which is connected to cups, symbolizes feelings and emotions. Cups are all about relationships, both with others and with ourselves. It is through our relationships that we learn and grow. We learn about love, compassion, and forgiveness. We also learn about anger, jealousy, and pain. Ultimately, we understand who we are and what we are here to do through our relationships.

The path of Netzach is the path of the heart. It is a path of love, compassion, and forgiveness. It is a path of healing and transformation. When we walk this path, we open ourselves up to limitless possibilities. We allow ourselves to be guided by our hearts and find our way back to our true nature.

Unlocking Netzach

To unlock Netzach Sephirah, you must have completed the previous five Sephiroth. Once you have done that, you can access

Netzach by meditating on the path between Binah and Chesed. When you reach Netzach, you will experience a sense of bliss and ecstasy. You may also see visions of lovely gardens or hear divine music. The key to unlocking Netzach is simply relaxing and letting yourself be open to whatever experiences come your way.

Meditation

To begin meditation, find a comfortable place to sit or lie down. Close your eyes and take a few deep breaths. Then, visualize yourself standing at the base of a great tree. This tree is the Tree of Life, and it represents your journey toward wholeness and enlightenment.

See yourself climbing the tree until you reach the fifth Sephirah, Binah. Then, continue up to the sixth Sephirah, Chesed. At Chesed, you will find a doorway leading into a beautiful garden. This is the Garden of Netzach.

Enter the garden and let yourself explore. Notice the sights, sounds, and smells around you. Listen to the birds singing and the breeze rustling through the leaves. Feel the sun on your skin and the grass beneath your feet.

As you explore the garden, you will come across a rosebush. Pluck a rose from the bush and hold it close to your heart. The rose is a symbol of Netzach Sephirah. It represents love, compassion, and beauty. As you hold the rose close to your heart, feel these qualities opening up within you.

Allow yourself to be filled with the energy of Netzach. Feel it flowing through you, around you, and within you. Listen to your heart's guidance, and let it lead you on your journey. When you are ready, begin to make your way back to the tree. Climb down the tree until you reach the ground. Then, open your eyes and return to the present moment.

Yesod - The Foundation

The Yesod Sephirah, also known as the Foundation, is the ninth and final sephirah on the Tree of Life. It is situated at the bottom of the tree, beneath the Malkuth sephirah. Yesod represents our connection to the physical world and serves as a foundation for all other sephiroth. It is associated with the Moon, which reflects the light of the Sun down to Earth.

The Yesod sephirah is also associated with memory, as it helps us to remember our past lives and experiences. Without Yesod, we would be lost in an ocean of forgetfulness. This sephirah also helps us to connect with our higher selves and access our higher consciousness. From Yesod, we can get a greater understanding of who we are and why we are here.

The Yesod Sephirah is also known as the "gateway to paradise" or the "gateway to truth." It is said to represent our connection to the divine and to be the source of all spiritual knowledge. The Yesod Sephirah is also associated with several other concepts, including balance, justice, righteousness, and integrity. As such, it is considered to be an important symbol in many different spiritual traditions.

Symbolism

The Yesod sephirah is symbolized by a cube. This is because it represents our connection to the physical world. The cube also symbolizes stability, as it has four equal sides and four equal corners. This stability helps us to remain grounded in our physical bodies and anchored in the present moment.

The color associated with Yesod is purple, the color of royalty. It represents our divine connection to the Source. Purple also symbolizes wisdom, as it is the color of the Third Eye Chakra. When we are attuned to our Third Eye Chakra, we can see beyond the physical world and access our higher consciousness.

Unlocking Yesod

Yesod can be unlocked through meditation and prayer. When we meditate on Yesod, we connect with our higher selves and access our spiritual knowledge. We can also unlock this sephirah by spending time in nature, as it helps us to remember our connection to the Earth. Furthermore, we can use crystals and stones to attune ourselves to the Yesod sephirah. Some of the most powerful crystals for this purpose include amethyst, moonstone, and labradorite.

When we work with the Yesod sephirah, we access our higher consciousness and connect with our spiritual truth. We also remember our past lives and experiences, which helps us to understand our present situation. We can better understand who we are and why we are here from Yesod.

Malchut - The Kingdom

The Malchut sephirah, also known as the Kingdom, is the tenth and final sephirah on the Tree of Life. It is found at the bottom of the tree, beneath the Yesod sephirah. Malchut represents our connection to the physical world and serves as a foundation for all other sephiroth. It is associated with the element of Earth, which is the material foundation of our lives. The Malchut sephirah is also associated with the planet Saturn, which is the planet of structure and stability.

As the final sephirah on the Tree of Life, Malchut represents our journey back to the Source. It is the sephirah of return, and it reminds us that all things must come to an end. From Malchut, we learn about death and rebirth and the cyclical nature of life. We can also gain a greater understanding of our place in the universe.

Symbolism

A crown symbolizes the Malchut sephirah. This is because it represents our connection to the physical world. The crown also symbolizes our journey back to the Source, reminding us that we are all royalty in the eyes of the Divine. Malchut's color is green, representing growth, abundance, and fertility. Green is also the color of the Heart Chakra, which is associated with love and compassion.

Unlocking Malchut

In the Kabbalah, Malchut is the sephirah that represents the realm of earthly experience. Through our connection to Malchut, we interact with the physical world and manifest our desires. When we are cut off from Malchut, we become disconnected from our true purpose and lose sight of what is important. The good news is that it is possible to unlock Malchut and reconnect with our source of power. By meditating on the sephirah and performing certain rituals, we can open the door to a richer, more fulfilling existence and begin to experience the world in a whole new way.

When we meditate on Malchut, we connect with our higher selves and access our spiritual knowledge. Another way to unlock this sephirah is by spending time in nature, as it reminds us of our connection to the Earth. Not only can we use crystals and stones to attune ourselves to the Malchut sephirah, but doing so can also help improve our connection with the divine. Some of the most powerful crystals for this purpose include emerald, jade, and green tourmaline.

How Malchut Represents the Physical Plane

Kabbalah teaches that there are four planes of existence: the physical, emotional, mental, and spiritual. Each plane is represented by one of the sephirot or divine attributes. The physical plane is represented by Malchut, which means "kingdom." This is because the physical plane is the kingdom of matter, where things are solid and tangible. Mastering the physical plane requires learning how to control and use the material world in a way that benefits all. When we live in harmony with the physical plane, we can create a peaceful and just world that provides everything we need.

How Malchut Relates to the Other Sephirot

Malchut is often viewed as the lowest of the sephirot, but this is only because it is the last sephirah in the descending order. In reality, Malchut is just as important as any of the other sephirot. It represents the final stage of manifestation, where the spiritual energy of the other sephirot is condensed into physical form. Without Malchut, there would be no way to experience the divine on a physical level.

Malchut also is a bridge between the spiritual and physical worlds. Through Malchut, we can interact with the divine realm and receive guidance from Above. Finally, Malchut also represents our unique individuality. Each of us has a unique role to play in the world; through Malchut, we can express our uniqueness. Without Malchut, we would be indistinguishable from one another. As you can see, Malchut is a vital part of the cosmic order and plays an essential role in our lives.

The sephirot you have just covered are Hod, Netzach, and Yesod (from the Kabbalistic realm of Yetzirah) as well as Malchut (from Assiah, the physical realm). These four sephirot represent the last stage of manifestation, where the spiritual energy of the other sephirot is condensed into physical form. Each sephirah plays a vital role in our lives and helps us interact more deeply with the world.

Chapter 7: The Archangels of the Tree of Life

In Judaism, angels are regarded as the intermediaries between God and humanity. They are believed to play an important role in guiding and protecting people on their spiritual journeys. In Kabbalah, they are seen as reflections of different aspects of God and are thought to be messengers from the divine realm who bring mystical knowledge and insights. Angels are also sometimes invoked in Jewish prayers and rituals. For example, people often say that reading the Torah is like getting advice from an angel. In general, angels are considered powerful spiritual beings who can help us connect with the Divine.

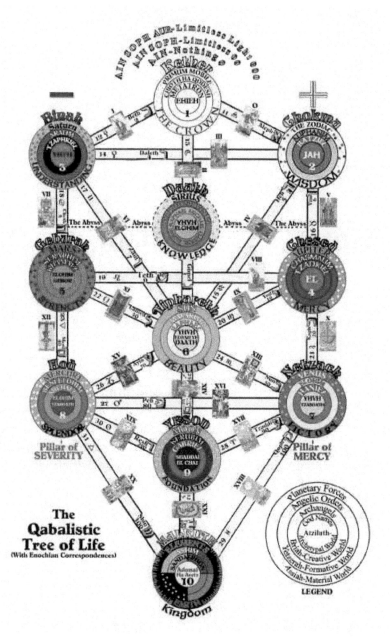

Each of the sephirot on the Tree of Life is represented by an archangel.

VendettaXIII, CC BY-SA 4.0 <https://creativecommons.org/licenses/by-sa/4.0>, via Wikimedia Commons: https://commons.wikimedia.org/wiki/File:Qabbalah-tree-of-life.jpg

Each of the sephirot on the Tree of Life is represented by an archangel. In this chapter, we will illustrate which angel belongs to which sphere. Then, we will go through each sephirah again, this time focusing only on the archangel that represents it. We will explain why that angelic being is connected to that sephirah, describe the characteristics of that archangel, their role as well as how they can help the reader, and lastly, include a short prayer dedicated to that archangel.

The Archangels of the Tree of Life

The Tree of Life, often seen as a connection between heaven and earth, represents the path we take through life. The archangels are powerful celestial beings who are said to watch over us as we travel along this path. There are ten archangels, each of whom is associated with one of the 10 sephirot on the Tree of Life. These include Metatron (Kether), Raziel (Chokmah), Tzaphkiel (Binah), Tzadkiel (Chesed), Kamael (Geburah), Raphael (Tipheret), Haneil (Netzach), Michael (Hod), Gabriel (Yesod), and Sandalphon (Malkuth).

The Archangel of Kether: Metatron

Kether, the highest sphere of the Tree of Life, is home to the Archangel Metatron. As the "Prince of Countenance," he is the angel who stands before the face of God. Metatron is said to be responsible for recording and maintaining all of God's thoughts and plans. He is also the angel who transmits God's will to humanity. In Jewish tradition, Metatron is sometimes called "the voice of God." In reality, he is the one who brings God and people together. Metatron is a powerful and influential figure in both Jewish and Christian mysticism. His name means "he who occupies the throne next to the Divine Throne." He is a very near and special Angel to God Himself.

Characteristics

Metatron is a powerful and wise being who serves as a guide and protector for humanity. Metatron is usually shown as a young man with wings holding a sword or a staff. He is also said to be very tall, with a shining countenance. Some traditions identify Metatron as the Angel of the Covenant or the Scribe of God. In Jewish tradition, he is known as the man who led Abraham out of Ur and into Canaan. In the New Testament, he is mentioned as the angel who appeared to Moses in the burning bush. Metatron is a powerful and wise being and a strong ally for those who want help and protection.

Role

Archangel Metatron is the ruler of all the angels and the protector of all of God's secrets. He is also the scribe of God because it is said that he has recorded everything that has ever been written. Archangel Metatron is a powerful being often called upon to help us in our time of need. He is said to be able to manifest anything that we need, and he can also help us understand life's mysteries. When we call upon Archangel Metatron, we ask for his help to guide us on our path.

A Prayer to Metatron

Dear Archangel Metatron,

Thank you for your guidance and protection. You are a powerful being who knows all of God's secrets. Help us understand life's mysteries and manifest what we need. We call upon you in our time of need and ask that you help us find our way. Thank you for your wisdom and your strength.

Amen.

The Archangel of Chokmah: Raziel

Raziel is the archangel of wisdom and knowledge. Raziel is a powerful being who can help us to understand the hidden knowledge of the universe. He is said to be the keeper of all of God's secrets and is known as the "Angel of Mysteries." Raziel is often depicted as a man with wings, holding a book or scroll in his hand. In Jewish tradition, Raziel is known as the "Great Angel" or the "Prince of Angels." He is also said to be the angel who taught Adam and Eve about the secrets of life.

Characteristics

Raziel is the Archangel of Chokmah, the divine wisdom of God. He is often depicted as a powerful and radiant being shrouded in light. Raziel is known for his great wisdom and knowledge and is said to be a master of all spiritual mysteries. He is also a guide and teacher, helping souls to remember their true nature and purpose. Raziel is a fierce protector of the innocent and a powerful force for good. He is often called upon in times of trouble or crisis, and his presence can bring hope and comfort. He is a miraculous being, and his guidance can help us navigate life's challenges with grace and ease.

Role

Raziel represents wisdom and understanding. In Jewish tradition, Raziel is known as the angel of secrets and mysteries. Raziel is also associated with the element of water. This is fitting, as water is often seen as a symbol of knowledge and understanding. In many traditions, Raziel is also known as the angel of judgment. This is because he is said to preside over the weighing of souls in the afterlife. As the Archangel of Chokmah, Raziel represents all that is wise and intelligent in the universe. He is a powerful ally for those seeking to understand existence's secrets.

Prayer to Raziel

Dear Archangel Raziel,

Thank you for your wisdom and guidance. You are the keeper of all of God's secrets and master of all spiritual mysteries. Help us to remember our true nature and purpose, and lead us on our path with grace and ease. We call upon you in times of trouble or crisis and know that your presence will bring us comfort and hope. Thank you for your compassion and your wisdom.

Amen.

The Archangel of Binah: Tzaphkiel

Tzaphkiel is the archangel of Binah, the third Sefira. Binah is associated with understanding, insight, and Wisdom, and Tzaphkiel is often invoked when seeking to gain knowledge or clarity. He is also known as the "Angel of Silence" because he infuses our hearts with Divine understanding. When we turn to Tzaphkiel for guidance, we open ourselves up to greater insight and understanding. In doing so, we align ourselves more closely with the Divine Will.

Characteristics

Binah is understanding, and Tzaphkiel helps us to understand ourselves and the world around us. He is also the angel of "divine will" and can help us to align our own will with that of the Divine. Tzaphkiel has a calm and gentle energy and is a great angel to call upon when we need clarity and guidance. He can also help us to let go of negative patterns and behaviors that no longer serve us. Call on Tzaphkiel, the kind archangel of Binah, if you want to understand your life or get help with it.

Role

Tzaphkiel helps us to see both the eternal and temporal aspects of reality and to understand their relationships to one another. Tzaphkiel also helps us reach the higher levels of consciousness we need to grow spiritually. One of the most crucial things that Tzaphkiel teaches us is that everything is connected. Everything that exists in the universe is interrelated, and it is only through understanding these relationships that we can achieve true wisdom. Tzaphkiel also reminds us that love is the most powerful force in the universe. When we open our hearts to love, we can tap into a vast reservoir of power and wisdom. By following Tzaphkiel's teachings, we can learn to live in harmony with all of creation.

Prayer to Tzaphkiel

Dear Archangel Tzaphkiel,

Thank you for your guidance and wisdom. You are the angel of understanding and help us see the interconnectedness of all things. You teach us that everything is connected and that love is the most powerful force in the universe. Help us to align our will with the Divine Will, and lead us on our path with grace and ease.

Amen.

The Archangel of Chesed: Tzadkiel

Archangel Tzadkiel is the Angel of Chesed or Loving-Kindness. He is called the "Prince of Mercy," and people often ask for his help when they need to forgive someone. Tzadkiel also presides over Wednesday, the day of Mercury. In Jewish tradition, Tzadkiel is also known as "Sachiel," and he is associated with the Sefirah of Netzach. In Kabbalah, Tzadkiel is seen as a powerful mediator between the Divine Will and human actions. He is said to bring our prayers before the Throne of Grace and is known for his ability to infuse our lives with Chesed. Archangel Tzadkiel is a potent force for good in the world, and he can be called upon for help in times of need.

Characteristics

The Archangel of Chesed, Tzadkiel, is known for his compassion and mercy. He is often invoked in times of trouble or hardship, as he is said to bring comfort and peace. Tzadkiel is also known for his ability to help us forgive ourselves and others and let go of emotions like anger, resentment, and bitterness. In Jewish tradition, Tzadkiel is associated with the sefirah of Chesed, which represents loving-kindness and compassion. Chesed is the divine quality that allows us to give and receive love unconditionally. It is the force that binds us together as a community and helps us to nurture and care for one another. Tzadkiel reminds us that we are all connected and that we each have the capacity for great love and compassion.

Role

In Jewish thought, Chesed is one of the highest virtues. It encompasses everything from compassion and mercy to forgiveness and generosity. Tzadkiel's role is to help us cultivate Chesed in our own lives. When we act with Chesed, we fulfill God's will and make the world better. As well as being the angel of Chesed, Tzadkiel is also associated with tzedakah or charity. He reminds us that we must help those less fortunate than ourselves. By giving our time, energy, and resources, we can make a real difference in the lives of others. Following Tzadkiel's example, we can learn to be more compassionate and caring.

Prayer to Tzadkiel

Dear Archangel Tzadkiel,

Thank you for your mercy and compassion. You are the angel of Chesed, and you remind us that we are all connected. You teach us the importance of giving and receiving love unconditionally. Help us to open our hearts to Chesed, and lead us on our path with grace and ease.

Amen.

The Archangel of Geburah: Kamael

Kamael is the Archangel of Geburah, one of the seven primary Archangels who rule over the Seven Heavens. He is known as the "Sovereign of Justice" and is said to dispense divine retribution. Kamael is also associated with strength, courage, and fortitude. He is often illustrated as carrying a sword or wielding a lightning bolt. Some believe that Kamael fell from grace after refusing to bow down to humans. As a result, he was cast out of Heaven and became the ruler of Hell. However, other stories say that Kamael remains in Heaven, protecting those who have been wronged. No matter his current whereabouts, Kamael is a powerful force for good and evil. He is a reminder that even the mightiest can fall but that redemption is always possible.

Characteristics

Kamael is the Archangel of Geburah, a powerful warrior and an avenging angel; he is known for his justice and righteousness. Kamael is also known as the "Slayer of Kings" and the "Destroyer of Worlds." He is a fierce opponent of evil and injustice, and he will not hesitate to fight against those who threaten the peace and harmony of the Universe. Kamael is a powerful ally in the fight against evil, and he will stand with those who are righteous and just. He is a force for good in the world and will help those who seek to do right. Kamael is a friend to all who are good and an enemy to all who are evil. He is the Archangel of Geburah and will always fight for what is right.

Role

According to angelic lore, the archangel Kamael is the ruler of the fifth heaven and one of the Seven Archangels who stand before the throne of God. As the Archangel of Geburah, Kamael represents strength, power, and judgment. In Jewish tradition, Kamael is often equated with Samael, the Angel of Death. However, in other belief systems, Kamael is considered a force for good, helping protect humanity from evil forces. Whether seen as a bringer of death or a defender of life, the Archangel Kamael is an important figure in many spiritual traditions.

Prayer to Kamael

Dear Archangel Kamael,

Thank you for your strength and courage. You are the Archangel of Geburah, and you dispense divine justice. You are a powerful ally in the fight against evil and will always fight for what is right. Help us to stand against injustice and evil, and lead us to a life of peace and harmony.

Amen.

The Archangel of Tiphareth: Raphael

Raphael is the Archangel of Tiphareth, the fifth Sephirah on the Tree of Life. He is known as the "healing angel" and is associated with green and pink colors. Raphael is often shown with a staff or wand in his hand, and a six-winged seraph is his symbol. Raphael's job as the Archangel of Tiphareth is to help souls reach their highest potential. He helps us to tap into our creativity and bliss and brings healing energy into our lives. When we call upon Raphael, we open ourselves up to receive his guidance and support. In doing so, we can create more harmonious lives for ourselves and those around us.

Characteristics

Raphael is one of the most important archangels in Judaism, Christianity, and Islam. He is known as the "angel of healing" or the "angel of hope." Raphael is often shown holding a staff or a scroll. He is also associated with the sun and with the color green. In the Book of Tobit, Raphael disguised himself as a man and helped Tobias to find a wife and cure his father's blindness. In the Bible, Raphael is one of the seven archangels standing before God's throne. In Islam, Raphael is known as Israfil and is responsible for blowing the trumpet on Judgment Day. Raphael is a powerful and benevolent angel who can help us in times of need.

Role

Raphael is associated with the element of air; his name means "healing" or "medicine" in Hebrew. Raphael is often depicted holding a staff or wand, which represents his power to heal, and he is also known as the Angel of Deliverance. He is a powerful ally for anyone seeking physical and emotional healing and can also help protect against disease. Raphael is also known for bringing peace and harmony, and people often call on him when there is trouble. Whether you are seeking healing for yourself or someone else, calling on Raphael can help to bring about positive change.

Prayer to Raphael

Dear Archangel Raphael,

Thank you for your healing energy. You are the Angel of Deliverance and bring hope and healing into our lives. You are associated with the element of air and help us breathe life into our dreams. You guide us toward our highest potential and help us create more harmonious lives.

Amen.

The Archangel of Netzach: Haniel

Haniel is the angel of beauty, inspiration, and grace. Her name means "glory of God," and she is usually shown with a bouquet or a crystal orb in her hands. As the Archangel of Netzach, Haniel governs the seventh chakra, which is associated with the colors pink and green. Haniel helps us to connect with our higher selves and tap into our creative potential. She is a powerful ally in times of Transition when we seek guidance on our life path. Haniel's energy is feminine and receptive, and she reminds us that sometimes the best thing to do is just to let our dreams and desires come true when they are ready. When we call on Haniel, we open ourselves up to a world of possibility.

Characteristics

Haniel is the Archangel of Netzach, the seventh Sephira on the Tree of Life. Netzach represents the spiritual victory over the material, and Haniel helps us achieve this victory. Haniel is often associated with the planet Venus; her name means "glory" or "grace." She brings us beauty, sweetness, and love. Haniel also helps us to connect with our higher selves and our Angels. We can call on Haniel to help us achieve our goals and manifest our desires. Haniel's energy is feminine and receptive, and we can call on Haniel to help us balance our masculine and feminine energies. She is a powerful ally in our spiritual journey.

Role

The Archangel of Netzach is Haniel. Netzach is the seventh sephira on the Tree of Life. It is situated at the bottom right of the tree and is represented by the planet Venus. The name Netzach means "victory" or "eternity." It is also associated with the concepts of love, beauty, and nature. As the Archangel of Netzach, Haniel is responsible for helping us to connect with these qualities. She helps us to see the beauty in all things and appreciate the natural world around us. Haniel also inspires us to pursue our dreams and never give up. No matter what challenges we face, Haniel reminds us that we have the inner strength to overcome them and achieve our goals.

Prayer to Haniel

Dear Archangel Haniel,

Thank you for your guidance and inspiration. You are the Angel of Netzach, and you help us to see the beauty in all things. You are associated with the planet Venus, and you bring us love, beauty, and harmony. Thank you for your help in bringing more balance into our lives.

Amen.

The Archangel of Hod: Michael

The Archangel of Hod, Michael, is known for his strength and power. He is one of the most popular angels in Catholicism and Christianity and is often depicted as a powerful warrior. In the Bible, Michael is described as the leader of God's army and said to have defeated Satan in a battle in heaven. In addition to his role as a protector, Michael is also known as the Angel of Healing. He is said to bring comfort to those who are suffering and provide them with strength in times of need. For Christians, Michael is a powerful symbol of hope and protection, and his image can be found in churches around the world.

Characteristics

Archangel Michael is the Archangel of Hod, which means "Glory." He is associated with protection, healing, and salvation. As the Archangel of Hod, Michael is responsible for helping us to manifest our highest potential. He is also known as the Prince of Angels and is considered the leader of the archangels. Archangel Michael is said to be the most powerful of all the archangels. He is often depicted holding a sword or wearing armor. He is also associated with the color blue. Archangel Michael can help you to connect with your higher self, heal old wounds, and protect yourself from negative energy. If you are seeking guidance or protection, Archangel Michael can help you to find your way.

Role

Archangel Michael is the archangel of protection, strength, and courage. He is known as the defender of the faith and the patron saint of policemen and soldiers. Archangel Michael is also known as the Prince of Angels and the leader of God's army. He is often depicted holding a sword or wearing armor. Archangel Michael is a powerful intercessor and protector. He is invoked for protection from danger, disease, and violence. Archangel Michael also helps us to let go of fear, worry, and doubt. He fills us with strength, courage, and peace when we call on him.

Prayer to Archangel Michael

Dear Archangel Michael,

Thank you for your protection and guidance. You are the Archangel of Hod, and you help us to manifest our highest potential. You are the leader of the archangels and the patron saint of policemen and soldiers. Thank you for filling us with strength, courage, and peace when we call on you.

Amen.

The Archangel of Yesod: Gabriel

Of all the archangels, Gabriel is perhaps the best known. He is the angel of revelation and delivered the news of Jesus' birth to the Virgin Mary. In addition, Gabriel is also associated with the Moon card in tarot readings. This card represents new beginnings, emotional depths, and hidden truths. Gabriel can be seen as a symbol of divine guidance and spiritual inspiration. So whatever your goal or challenge may be, remember that you can always call on Gabriel to help achieve it.

Characteristics

The Archangel of Yesod is Gabriel. He stands at the gate of Eden, and his task is to keep the way of the Tree of Life clear for humanity. He is also responsible for guiding souls to their proper place in the afterlife. Gabriel is a powerful angel; his strength lies in his ability to help others. He is a guardian angel, and he will protect those who are under his care. He is also a teacher and will help those who want to learn about the Tree of Life. Gabriel is a kind and compassionate angel who will always be there to help those who need it.

Prayer to Archangel Gabriel

Dear Archangel Gabriel,

Thank you for your guidance and protection. You are the Archangel of Yesod, and you are responsible for keeping the way of the Tree of Life clear for humanity. You are a guardian angel, and you will protect those who are under your care. You are also a teacher and will help those who want to learn about the Tree of Life.

Amen.

The Archangel of Malkuth: Sandalphon

Sandalphon is the Archangel of Malkuth, the tenth and final sephira on the Tree of Life. He is called the "messenger of God" and is often shown holding a scroll or a trumpet. Sandalphon is in charge of directing our prayers to Heaven and conveying Divine messages. He is also a protector of Earth and its creatures. In many ways, Sandalphon is the perfect guardian angel for our world. He is committed to assisting us in finding a happy medium between them. If we ever feel lost or disconnected from the Divine, we can call on Sandalphon for guidance. He will help us find our way back home.

Characteristics

Sandalphon is known as the "Heavenly Scribe," and he is responsible for communicating our prayers to God. He is also known as the "Angel of Music" because he helps us connect with the divine melodies of the universe. Sandalphon is closely connected to Mother Earth; he helps us be grounded and anchor our energy in the physical world. He also helps us connect with our ancestors and the wisdom of our elders. Sandalphon is a powerful Archangel who can help us to manifest our desires and bring our prayers to fruition.

Prayer to Archangel Sandalphon

Dear Archangel Sandalphon,

Thank you for your guidance and protection. You are the Archangel of Malkuth and are responsible for guiding our prayers to Heaven. You are also a protector of the Earth and its creatures. In many ways, you are the perfect guardian angel for our world. You understand both the material and spiritual realms and are dedicated to helping us find a balance between them.

Amen.

The Archangels play an important role in Judaism mysticism and Kabbalah. They are responsible for guiding our prayers up to Heaven, delivering messages from the Divine, and protecting us from harm. They are also powerful symbols of divine guidance and spiritual inspiration. So whatever your goal or challenge may be, remember that you can always call on the Archangels to help achieve it.

Chapter 8: The Twenty-Two Paths and Major Arcana

For several reasons, Hebrew is considered to be a divine or mystical language. The language is unique in that it is alphabetical and also pictographic. In other words, each letter of the Hebrew alphabet is not only a letter but ***also a word and a concept.*** For example, the first letter of the Hebrew alphabet, Aleph, is also the word for "ox." This connection between the written and pictorial representations of words gives Hebrew a depth of meaning that other languages lack.

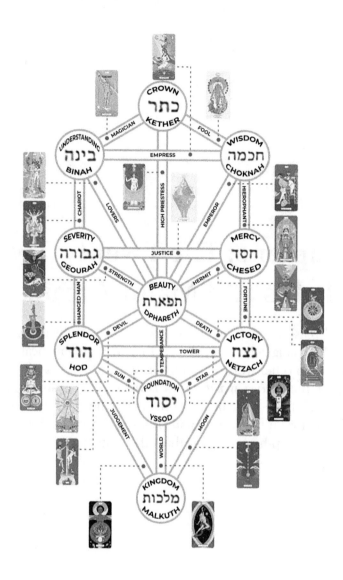

Each path has an association with a Major Arcana card.

This chapter will explore the connection between the Hebrew alphabet, the 22 paths on the Tree of Life, and the 22 Major Arcana cards in tarot. We will go through each path and explain its symbolism and association with its corresponding Major Arcana card.

The Hebrew Alphabet and the Tree of Life

The Hebrew Alphabet is a mystical tool that has been used for centuries to unlock the Universe's secrets. Tradition says that each letter of the alphabet represents a different level of reality and that by meditating on the letters, one can learn about the hidden parts of life. The Tree of Life is a central symbol in Hebrew mysticism, and it is said that the letters of the alphabet are like the branches of the tree, with each one leading to a different level of understanding.

In recent years, scientists have begun exploring the potential links between the Hebrew Alphabet and quantum physics, and many believe that this ancient system is the key to unlocking the mysteries of our Universe. Whether you are a seeker of knowledge or just curious about the mysteries of life, the Hebrew Alphabet is sure to offer you new insights and understanding.

The 22 Paths and the Major Arcana

Like many of the world's great religions, the tree of life is a symbol of rebirth and growth. The tree of life has 22 paths, representing the tarot's major arcana. Each path leads to a different destination, and each destination has its meaning. For example, the first path leads to the gates of paradise, while the last path leads to the underworld. In between, some paths represent love, death, and redemption. The Tree of Life is a beautiful symbol of the journey we all take. It is a reminder that there is always hope for growth and change. Whether at the beginning or the end of our journey, we can always find new paths to explore.

1. The Path of Aleph and the Fool

The Path of Aleph is the first path on the Tree of Life, representing new beginnings. This path connects the sephirot of Kether and Chokmah, and its symbolic meaning is primal energy. The Fool is often associated with this path, as this card is about taking risks and embracing the unknown. The Fool can also represent change and transformation.

2. The Path of Beth and the Magician

The second path on the Tree of Life is the Path of Beth, which represents knowledge and understanding. It connects the sephirot of

Kether and Binah, and its symbolic meaning is attention. This path is often linked to The Magician because this card is about using your knowledge and skills to make your own reality. The Magician is also a symbol of resourcefulness and creativity.

3. The Path of Gimel and the High Priestess

The third path on the Tree of Life is the Path of Gimel, which represents intuition and wisdom. The Path of Gimel connects the sephirot of Kether and Tiphereth and is symbolic of receptivity. The High Priestess is often associated with this path, as she symbolizes intuition and mystery. The High Priestess also reminds us that we all have access to hidden knowledge.

4. The Path of Daleth and the Empress

The fourth path on the Tree of Life is the Path of Daleth, which represents fertility and creation. The Path of Daleth connects the sephirot of Chokmah and Binah and is associated with nourishment. Since the Empress is a symbol of motherhood and femininity, it is often linked to this path. The Empress also reminds us that we are all connected to the natural world.

5. The Path of Heh and the Emperor

The Path of Heh, representing authority and structure, is the fifth path on the Tree of Life. The Path of Heh connects the sephirot of Chokmah and Tiphereth and is associated with reasoning. The Emperor is often linked to this path, as it is a symbol of strength and stability. The Emperor also reminds us that we all have the power to create our own rules and boundaries.

6. The Path of Vav and the Hierophant

The Path of Vav is the sixth path on the Tree of Life, representing balance and harmony. The Path of Vav connects the sephirot of Chokmah and Chesed and is associated with connections. The Hierophant is often linked to this path, as it symbolizes understanding and tradition. The Hierophant also reminds us that we are all part of a larger community.

7. The Path of Zain and the Lovers

The seventh path on the Tree of Life is the Path of Zain, which represents relationships and choices. The Path of Zain connects the sephirot of Binah and Tiphereth and is associated with discernment. The Lovers card is often linked to this path, as it is about making decisions based on our hearts. The Lovers is also a reminder that we are all connected.

8. The Path of Cheth and the Chariot

The eighth path on the Tree of Life is the Path of Cheth, which represents victory and success. The Path of Cheth connects the sephirot of Binah and Geburah and is associated with a field. The Chariot is often linked to this path, as it is a symbol of triumph. The Chariot is also a reminder that we all have the power to achieve our goals.

9. The Path of Teth and the Strength

The Path of Teth is the ninth path on the Tree of Life, representing courage and strength. The Path of Teth links the sephirot of Geburah to that of Tiphereth, and it is related to willpower. Strength is often linked to this path, as it is a card about using our inner strength to overcome obstacles. Strength is also a reminder that we are all capable of overcoming challenges.

10. The Path of Yod and the Hermit

The Path of Yod is the tenth path on the Tree of Life, which is all about introspection and contemplation. The Path of Yod connects the sephirot of Chesed and Tipareth and is associated with deed and work. The Hermit is often linked to this path, as it is a symbol of solitude and reflection. The Hermit also reminds us that we all need time to connect with our higher selves.

11. The Path of Kaph and the Wheel of Fortune

The Path of Kaph is the eleventh path on the Tree of Life, representing change and luck. The Path of Kaph connects the sephirot of Chesed and Netzach, and it is associated with a wheel. The Wheel of Fortune is often linked to this path, symbolizing life's ups and downs. The Wheel of Fortune is also a reminder that we all experience highs and lows, but we always have the power to change our circumstances.

12. The Path of Lamed and the Justice

The twelfth path on the Tree of Life is the Path of Lamed, which represents balance and fairness. The Path of Lamed is associated with balance and connects the sephirot of Geburah and Chesed. Justice is often linked to this path, as it is a symbol of making sure that we are living our lives in a way that is fair to ourselves and others. Justice also reminds us that we all have the power to create our destiny.

13. The Path of Mem and the Hanged Man

The thirteenth path on the Tree of Life is the Path of Mem, which represents sacrifice and surrender. The Path of Mem connects the sephirot of Geburah and Hod, and it is associated with water. The Hanged Man is often linked to this path, as it symbolizes letting go and being open to change. The Hanged Man is also a reminder that we all have the power to let go of our past and start fresh.

14. The Path of Nun and Death

The fourteenth path on the Tree of Life is the Path of Nun, which represents transformation and rebirth. The Path of Nun connects the sephirot of Tiphareth and Netzach, and it is associated with a fish. Death is often linked to this path, as it is a symbol of transformation and new beginnings. Death is a lesson that we all can let go of our past selves and begin anew.

15. The Path of Samech and Temperance

The fifteenth path on the Tree of Life is the Path of Samech, which represents moderation and balance. The Path of Samech connects the sephirot of Tiphareth and Yesod and is associated with an hourglass. Temperance is often linked to this path, as it symbolizes finding balance in our lives. Temperance also reminds us that we all have the power to create our destiny.

16. The Path of Ayin and the Devil

The sixteenth path on the Tree of Life is the Path of Ayin, which represents temptation and materialism. The Path of Ayin connects the sephirot of Tiphareth and Hod, and it is associated with a snake. The Devil is often linked to this path, as it is a symbol of our darker side. The Devil is also a reminder that we all have the power to resist temptation and stay on the path of righteousness.

17. The Path of Peh and the Tower

The Path of Peh is the seventeenth path on the Tree of Life, representing destruction and chaos. The Path of Peh connects the sephirot of Netzach and Hod, and it is associated with a lightning bolt. The Tower is often linked to this path, as it symbolizes our need to face our fears head-on. The Tower is also a reminder that we all have the power to overcome our fears and rise above them.

18. The Path of Tzaddi and the Star

The eighteenth path on the Tree of Life is the Path of Tzaddi, which represents hope and guidance. The Path of Tzaddi connects the sephirot of Netzach and Yesod, and it is associated with an anchor. The Star is often linked to this path, as it is a symbol of hope and guidance. The Star is also a reminder that we all have the power to find our way in life, no matter how lost we feel.

19. The Path of Qoph and the Moon

The nineteenth path on the Tree of Life is the Path of Qoph, representing illusion and deception. The Path of Qoph connects the sephirot of Netzach and Malkuth and is associated with hiding. The Moon is often linked to this path, symbolizing our ability to see through the illusions in life. The Moon is also a reminder that we all have the power to find our way in life, no matter how dark or chaotic it may seem.

20. The Path of Resh and the Sun

The eighteenth path on the Tree of Life is the Path of Resh, which represents enlightenment and happiness. The Path of Resh connects the sephirot of Hod and Yesod, and it is associated with redemption. The Sun is often linked to this path, as it symbolizes our ability to find joy amid the darkness. The Sun is also a reminder that we all have the power to find our inner light and let it shine forth.

21. The Path of Shin and Judgment

The nineteenth path on the Tree of Life is the Path of Shin, which represents rebirth and new beginnings. The Path of Shin connects the sephirot of Hod and Malkuth, and it is associated with a fire. Judgment is often linked to this path, as it symbolizes our ability to start anew – and it also reminds us that we all have the power to create our destiny.

22. The Path of Taw and the World

The twentieth path on the Tree of Life is the Path of Taw, which represents completion and fulfillment. The Path of Taw connects the sephirot of Malkuth and Yesod and is associated with truth. The World is often linked to this path, as it symbolizes our ability to find wholeness and completion. The World is also a reminder that we all have the power to create our reality.

Kabbalistic Tarot Reading: Reversed Cards

If you pull a reversed tarot card, it means that the energy of that card is currently blocked in your life. This can be interpreted in several ways, depending on which card you pull. For example, if you pull The Tower reversed, it could mean that you are currently facing some fears or challenges head-on. Alternatively, it could also mean that you are in the process of overcoming your fears. If you pull The Star reversed, it could mean that you are currently feeling lost or directionless. Alternatively, it could also mean that you are in the process of finding your way.

The reversed cards in your reading suggest you are not facing up to some of the challenges in your life. You may be feeling overwhelmed or stuck, and you may be avoiding difficult situations. The reversed cards also suggest that you are not seeing the whole picture and not taking all the available options into account. You may need to take a step back and reassess your situation. Look at things from a different perspective, and consider all of the possible outcomes. Be willing to make changes and take risks. The reversed cards indicate the potential for growth and transformation if you are willing to face your fears and take action.

The Tree of Life comprises 10 sephirot, which are connected by 22 paths. These paths are associated with the 22 letters of the Hebrew alphabet. The Tree of Life symbolizes our ability to find balance and harmony in our lives. The sephirot represent different aspects of our being, and the paths represent the journey we take to find wholeness. Each path has its own symbolism and meaning, which can be used to interpret the tarot. Tarot is a tool that can be used to help us understand the journey that we are on. This chapter has provided a brief overview of the Tree of Life and its connection to the tarot.

Chapter 9: The Tree of Life and Minor Arcana

In the previous chapter, we explored the Tree of Life and the Major Arcana cards associated with each of the sephirot. In this chapter, we will continue our exploration of the Tree of Life by looking at the Minor Arcana cards and their connections to the four worlds, the four elements, and the four suites. We will also discover how the sephirot correspond to the numerical values of the Minor Arcana cards. Finally, we will see how this kabbalistic method can be used for readings.

Assiah	Yetzirah	Beri'ah	Atziluth
World of Manifestation	World of Formation	World of Creation	World of Emanation
Body	Psyche	Spirit	Divine
Faculty of Sensation	Faculty of Thinking	Faculty of Feeling	Faculty of Intuition
ה	ו	ה	י
HE	VAU	HE	YOD
Pentacles	*Swords*	*Cups*	*Wands*
Earth	Air	Water	Fire

The Minor Arcana is a deck of tarot cards that represent the everyday challenges we face in life.

Tree of Life in Conjunction with Minor Arcana

The Tree of Life represents the interconnectedness of all life and how necessary balance is. The tree branches represent life's journey, while the leaves represent different parts of life. The roots represent our connection to the past, and the trunk represents our present self. The Tree of Life is also often used to symbolize the four stages of life: birth, growth, death, and rebirth.

The Minor Arcana is a deck of tarot cards that represent the everyday challenges we face in life. The Swords suit shows our thoughts and mental challenges, and the Wands suit shows our actions and physical challenges. The suit of Cups represents our emotional challenges, while the suit of Pentacles represents our material and financial challenges. Each one contains fourteen cards, divided into four groups: Ace through Ten, Page, Knight, and Queen. These groups represent the different stages of life: birth (Ace), growth (Page), death (Knight), and rebirth (Queen).

When we look at the Tree of Life and Minor Arcana together, we can see that they both symbolize life's journey. The Tree of Life shows us that every stage of life is connected, and we must maintain a balance between all areas of our existence. The Minor Arcana reminds us that challenges are a natural part of life and that we must face them head-on to grow and learn. Together, these symbols can help us navigate life's ups and downs with wisdom and grace.

The Four Worlds

The Tree of Life is divided into four worlds: Assiah, Yetzirah, Briah, and Atziluth. Each of these worlds is associated with a different element. Assiah is the world of manifestation, and its element is Earth. Yetzirah is the world of formation and is associated with the element of air. Briah is the world of creation, fire is its element, and Atziluth is the world of emanation. It is associated with the element of water.

Each of the four worlds is also associated with a different suite of Minor Arcana cards. Assiah is linked to the suit of Pentacles, Yetzirah to the suit of Swords, Briah to the suit of Wands, and Atziluth to the suit of Cups.

The Four Elements

The Tree of Life is also divided into four elements: fire, water, air, and earth. The four suits of the Minor Arcana, Wands (fire), Cups (water), Swords (air), and Pentacles (earth), represent these four elements. Each element is associated with a different stage of life: fire is associated with birth, water is associated with growth, the air is associated with death, and earth is associated with rebirth.

The Four Suites

The Minor Arcana is divided into four suites: Swords, Wands, Cups, and Pentacles. Each of these suites is connected to a different world: the Swords are connected to Assiah, the Wands to Yetzirah, the Cups to Briah, and the Pentacles to Atziluth.

The Sephirot and the Numerical Correspondences of the Minor Arcana

In the Kabbalistic tradition, the Sephirot are 10 emanations of the Divine that represent different aspects of God's nature. Each Sephirah has its own symbol and numerical correspondence, and these correspondences can be used to unlock the hidden meanings of the Minor Arcana in a Tarot reading. The first Sephirah, Kether, is linked with the number one and represents the Divine will or purpose. The second Sephirah, Chokmah, is associated with the number two and represents wisdom or understanding.

The third Sephirah, Binah, is coupled with the number three, representing knowledge or understanding. The fourth Sephirah, Chesed, is connected with the number four, representing mercy or compassion, while the fifth Sephirah, Geburah, is associated with the number five and represents strength or power.

The sixth Sephirah, Tiphareth, is associated with the number six and represents beauty or balance. Netzach, the seventh Sephirah, is associated with the number seven and represents victory or triumph. The eighth Sephirah, Hod, is associated with the number eight and represents glory or splendor.

The ninth Sephirah, Yesod, is associated with the number nine and represents foundation or stability. The tenth and final Sephirah, Malkuth, is associated with the number ten and represents kingdom or domain.

Example Readings

When you understand the meaning of each Sephirah, you can begin to see how the numerical correspondences of the Minor Arcana can be used to interpret the hidden meanings of a Tarot reading.

For example, if you are using a Swords-based deck and draw the Ace of Swords, this card would represent the Divine will or purpose (Kether) manifesting in the world of form (Assiah).

Suppose you use a Cups-based deck and draw the Ace of Cups. This card would represent the Divine will or purpose (Kether) manifesting in the world of emotion or feeling (Briah). In a reading, this card could indicate that you are about to experience a great influx of emotions or that you are about to embark on a new emotional journey.

If you are using a Wands-based deck, and you draw the Ace of Wands, this card would represent the Divine will or purpose (Kether) manifesting in the world of formation (Yetzirah). In a reading, these cards would indicate that something new is about to enter your life and that you have the power to shape it according to your own will.

The Tree of Life is a powerful tool for understanding the hidden meanings of the Tarot. By studying the Sephirot and their numerical correspondences, you can unlock the secrets of the Minor Arcana and gain a deeper insight into their role in a Tarot reading.

Chapter 10: Daily Kabalistic Rituals and Ideas

Kabbalah is a system of esoteric knowledge that includes principles and practices designed to help people achieve union with the divine. The Tree of Life is a central symbol in Kabbalah, representing the structure of the cosmos and the path that leads to ultimate reality. Kabbalists believe that the Tree of Life is a map of reality and a blueprint for creation. The Tree of Life is a symbol of the interconnectedness of all things. It is said to contain all the secrets of the universe. Kabbalists also believe the Tree of Life is a tool for spiritual growth, and by studying it, we can learn how to create our reality.

The Shabbat is also a time for performing special rituals, such as lighting candles and saying blessings over bread and wine.

https://www.pexels.com/photo/close-up-photo-of-candle-holder-on-top-of-glass-table-6115411/

Practicing Kabbalah can help us connect with the Divine and to lead more meaningful and productive lives. Many different Kabbalistic rituals and ideas can be incorporated into our daily lives. This chapter will explore some of the most popular Kabbalistic practices. It will also guide you through the ideal way to read and study the sacred texts of Kabbalah. With this knowledge, you'll be able to start incorporating Kabbalistic principles into your own life and begin your journey toward spiritual growth.

Daily Kabalistic Rituals and Ideas

Keeping the Kabbalistic Tree of Life in mind when performing your daily rituals is crucial. The Tree of Life is a representation of the universe, and by understanding its components, you can better understand the universe's workings and apply them to your own life. There are 10 Sephiroth on the Tree of Life, each representing a different aspect of existence. By meditating on these and including them in your daily rituals, you'll begin to imbue your life with the wisdom of the Kabbalah.

Some things to keep in mind when performing your rituals:

1. Always start with the Sephirah at the bottom of the tree and work your way up.
2. Make sure your thoughts and actions are aligned with each Sephirah.
3. Be patient and diligent in your practice; it may take time to see results.
4. Enjoy the journey, and let the wisdom of the Kabbalah guide you on your path.

The following are some daily rituals and ideas that you can incorporate into your life:

The Morning Prayer

The morning prayer is a great way to start the day with the Kabalistic Tree of Life in mind. By consecrating each day with this prayer, we begin to infuse our days and lives with the wisdom of the Kabbalah. The morning prayer is as follows:

"Blessed are You, Lord our God, King of the universe, who has sanctified us with His commandments and commanded us to pray.

God, in Your goodness, please incline Your ear and hear my prayer.

I arise today through Your grace and power. May I be filled with love and compassion for all living creatures? Let me perform good deeds today that will bring me closer to You. Help me to see the good in everyone I meet, and let me always be forgiving. Guide my thoughts and actions so that I may always do that which is pleasing unto You. Amen."

The Evening Prayer

One of the most important ways to connect with the wisdom of the Kabalistic tree of life is by performing daily rituals that honor its teachings. One such ritual is the evening prayer. This prayer helps to align oneself with the energy of the day and sets the tone for a peaceful and productive evening.

You will need a piece of paper and a pen or pencil to perform the evening prayer. Begin by sitting comfortably and taking a few deep breaths to calm your mind. Once you are relaxed, write down the following words:

"Dear God, thank you for this day and all it has brought. Thank you for your love, guidance, and protection. Please help me to align myself with your will for this evening. Amen."

Once you have written down the prayer, take a few minutes to focus on each word and what it means to you. As you do, open yourself up to feel the peace and calm that comes from connecting with God. When you are finished, fold up the paper and place it somewhere near your bed, where you can see it before going to sleep.

The Shabbat

The Shabbat is a special day of rest and contemplation in the Jewish tradition. It begins at sundown on Friday night and lasts until nightfall on Saturday. During this time, Jews refrained from work and devoted themselves to prayer, study, and spending time with family and friends. The Shabbat is also a time for performing special rituals, such as lighting candles and saying blessings over bread and wine.

These rituals help to create a sense of peace and tranquility, which can be especially beneficial during times of stress or turmoil. They also serve as a reminder of how necessary it is to slow down and take time to appreciate the simplest things in life. For Jews, the Shabbat is a sacred day – meant to be enjoyed and savored.

The New Moon

The New Moon is a time of new beginnings and the perfect time to perform some daily Kabalistic rituals. One simple ritual is to light a white candle and visualize your highest goal. As you focus on your intention, allow the candle's flame to represent the power of your desire. Another ritual is to write down your goals for the month ahead. Be specific and realistic in your intentions, and then let go of any attachment to the outcome.

Trust that the universe will support you in achieving your goals. Lastly, take some time on the New Moon to meditate and connect with your inner wisdom. Listen for guidance from your higher self, and trust that you are being supported on your journey. By taking some time to connect with the energy of the New Moon, you can set yourself up for success in the month ahead.

Passover

The Passover holiday is a time for Kabbalists to reflect on their spiritual journey and connect with their higher selves. One of the ways they do this is through daily rituals that help them to attune to the energies of the universe. One such ritual is the Seder, a ceremonial meal with special foods and prayers.

The Seder helps Kabbalists to remember the importance of liberation, both physical and spiritual. Another important ritual is counting the Omer, which is 49 days of introspection and meditation. The Omer helps Kabbalists to connect with their power and focus on their goals. By participating in these daily rituals, Kabbalists can deepen their connection to the divine and create a more fulfilling life.

The High Holy Days

The High Holy Days are some of the most important days in the Kabalistic calendar. These days, Kabbalists perform special cleansing and purification rituals and ask for forgiveness from the Divine. The first of the High Holy Days is Rosh Hashanah, which marks the beginning of the Jewish New Year. On Rosh Hashanah, Kabbalists gather together to pray and meditate. They also perform a special ritual known as Tashlikh, in which they cast their sins into a body of water.

The second High Holy Day is Yom Kippur – or the Day of Atonement. On Yom Kippur, Kabbalists fast and spend the day in prayer and contemplation. They also perform the rite of Kol Nidre, in which they repent for their past sins. These special rituals help Kabbalists to start the year anew with a clean slate and a deep connection to the Divine.

Sukkot

Sukkot is a seven-day festival that occurs in the fall. It is also known as the Feast of Tabernacles or the Feast of Ingathering. During Sukkot, Jews built temporary huts, or sukkahs, and ate all their meals inside them. The sukkah symbolizes the huts the Israelites lived in during their forty years in the desert.

Each day of Sukkot has its special rituals and observances. On the first day, Jews built their sukkahs and decorated them with fruits and vegetables. They also wave palm fronds and myrtle branches in six different directions, symbolizing the six directions of space. Special prayers and readings from the Torah are recited on the second day. On the third day, they offer sacrifices at the Temple in Jerusalem. And on the fourth day, they celebrate Hoshana Rabbah, which is when they praise God for His bountiful blessings.

Sukkot is a joyous occasion, but it is also a time for reflection. Jews remember their dependence on God's mercy and protection during this holiday. They also reflect on the importance of treating others with kindness and compassion. Sukkot is a time to celebrate our lives and all we have been blessed with while also remembering those less fortunate.

Daily Life with the Tree of Life

Meditation

We can use the Tree of Life as a guide for our daily meditation practice. For example, we can focus on one Sephira daily and meditate on its meaning and significance. Alternatively, we can choose to meditate on the path between two Sephiroth or on the entire Tree of Life itself. Kabalistic meditation is a powerful tool for self-discovery and growth, and the Tree of Life is an excellent map to help us on our journey.

Readings

Another way to permeate our daily lives with the grace of the Tree of Life is to select readings related to its symbolism and meaning. Many books are available, and Kabalistic texts often contain references to its Sephiroth. By reading about the Tree of Life, we get a deeper understanding of its wisdom and how it can help us to live more fulfilling lives.

Reciting Prayers

Prayer is a vital part of Kabalistic practice, and the Tree of Life can be a helpful guide for our prayer life. For example, we can recite prayers associated with specific Sephiroth or use the Tree of Life as a visualization tool during our prayers. We can deepen our connection to its wisdom and power by including the Tree of Life in our prayers.

Using the Tree of Life in the Creation of Future Goals

The Tree of Life can also be helpful to use when we want to set future goals. By understanding the symbolism of the Sephiroth, we can use them as guideposts on our journey toward our highest aspirations. By aligning our goals with the energies of the Tree of Life, we can increase our chances of achieving them.

Using the Kabbalistic System of Creation

The Kabbalistic creation system is useful for taking an idea from its raw, shapeless state (Keter) and transforming it into physical reality (Malkuth). Working through the ten Sephiroth stages of creation makes it possible to give form and substance to an idea, making it increasingly concrete and tangible. The ten Sephiroth is a hierarchy, with each stage building on the one before it. For example, the first stage, Keter, is the purest and most abstract form of an idea. As the idea moves down through the Sephiroth, it becomes increasingly refined and specific until it reaches Malkuth, the final stage, in which it takes on a physical form. Using the Kabbalistic system of creation, it is possible to bring even the most ephemeral idea into reality.

Sacred Kabbalistic Texts and How to Read Them

The Sefer Yetzirah

The Sefer Yetzirah is one of the most sacred texts in the Kabbalah tradition. It contains wisdom on how to create and interpret sacred Jewish texts. To read and understand the Sefer Yetzirah properly, it is crucial to have a basic understanding of the Hebrew alphabet. Each letter has a numerical value, which can be used to interpret the meaning of words and phrases. The Sefer Yetzirah also contains a great deal of symbolism, which can be difficult to interpret without guidance from a knowledgeable teacher. However, even a basic understanding of the text can provide insight into the depths of the Kabbalistic tradition. With proper study and practice, anyone can learn to read and understand the Sefer Yetzirah.

Zohar

There are many different sacred texts in the Jewish Kabbalistic tradition, and each has its unique purpose and teachings. The Zohar is perhaps the best-known and most studied of these texts – and is considered the *cornerstone of Kabbalistic wisdom.* The Zohar contains mystical secrets and insights into the nature of God, the universe, and the human soul. To properly understand and benefit from its teachings, it is necessary to approach the text with reverence and respect.

The Zohar is traditionally divided into five sections or books. Each section contains several chapters, or paragraphs, further divided into smaller units called paragraphs. In addition, each section has a specific color associated with it, which helps to guide the reader through the text. For example, the first book is connected with the color red, which symbolizes fire and passion. The second book is yellow, which represents wisdom and clarity. The third book is green, related to growth and fertility, while the fourth book is blue, connected with truth and understanding. Finally, the fifth book is purple, associated with royalty and power.

By taking the time to understand the structure and symbolism of the Zohar, readers can begin to unlock its secrets and gain deeper insight into its mystical teachings.

Bahir

The Bahir is a sacred text that has been used for centuries to help people connect with the divine. The word "Bahir" means "illumination," and the text is designed to help readers understand the universe and their place within it. It is divided into three sections, each of which contains a series of meditations, stories, and exercises. The first section, known as the "Practical Kabbalah," offers guidance on how to live a spiritual life.

The second section, known as the "Mystical Kabbalah," helps readers explore the nature of reality. The third section, known as the "Esoteric Kabbalah," helps readers understand the relationship between God and man. While the Bahir is not easy to read, it is considered essential for those who wish to deepen their understanding of the Kabbalah.

PaRDeS

The PaRDeS approach is a method of text interpretation that has its roots in Jewish Kabbalah. The acronym PaRDeS stands for four different levels of interpretation: peshat, remez, drash, and sod. Peshat is the text's literal meaning, while Remez is the allegorical meaning. Drash is the interpretive meaning, and sod is the hidden or mystical meaning. PaRDeS was first developed as a way to interpret sacred texts, but it can also be used when interpreting any type of written work.

When using the PaRDeS approach, readers first identify which level of interpretation they are looking for. They then read the text closely, looking for clues that will help them to unlock its meaning. Depending on the level they are aiming for, readers may need to look beyond the literal meaning of the words on the page and explore the hidden symbolism and allegorical meanings. By taking the time to unpack all four levels of interpretation, readers can gain a deeper understanding of any written work - from ancient religious texts to modern novels.

Kabbalah is a complex and mysterious tradition that religious scholars have studied for centuries. While it can be difficult to understand, the rewards for those who take the time to study it are great. By understanding the structure and symbolism of key Kabbalistic texts, such as the Zohar and the Bahir, readers can unlock the secrets of this ancient tradition and gain deeper insight into its teachings.

In addition, the PaRDeS approach to text interpretation can help readers understand any type of written work, from sacred texts to modern novels. By taking the time to explore all four levels of interpretation, readers can gain a greater understanding of the hidden meanings that lie beneath the surface of any text.

Extra: Glossary of Terms

Kabbalah is an ancient wisdom that reveals how to create harmony and balance in our lives. It is a system of knowledge that helps us to reach our highest potential and create the life we truly desire. This book introduced you to the basics of Kabbalah, its history, and how it can help you in your own life. This chapter will provide a brief glossary of terms for your convenience.

- **Ain Soph**: The Unknowable Godhead, the infinite light that is the source of all creation.
- **Ain Soph Aur:** The infinite light of God that is manifest in creation.
- **Atzilut:** The world of emanation, the highest of the four spiritual worlds.
- **Binah:** Understanding. In Kabbalah, Binah is the third sefirah and is considered the highest form of understanding.
- **Beriyah:** The world of creation, the second of the four spiritual worlds.
- **Butzina deKala:** The feminine aspect of God.
- **Chakra:** A spinning wheel of energy located in the body. There are 7 main chakras in the body, each associated with a different area and function.
- **Chesed:** Lovingkindness. In Kabbalah, Chesed is the fourth sefirah and is considered the highest expression of love.

- **Chokhmah**: Wisdom. In Kabbalah, Chokhmah is the second sefirah and is considered the highest form of wisdom.

- **Da'at:** Knowledge. In Kabbalah, Da'at is the tenth sefirah and is considered the highest form of knowledge. Through Da'at, we can attain a true understanding of the universe.

- **Ein Sof:** The unknowable Godhead, the infinite light that is the source of all creation. In Kabbalah, Ein Sof is often referred to as the "Ain Soph Aur" or the "Infinite Light of God."

- **Elyon:** The highest or most exalted one. In Kabbalah, Elyon refers to God as the supreme being who is above all else.

- **Gan Eden:** The Garden of Eden, the paradise that awaits us after we die.

- **Gehinnom:** The Jewish concept of hell.

- **Gevurah:** Strength or power. In Kabbalah, Gevurah is the fifth sefirah and is considered the highest expression of strength.

- **Hokhmah:** Wisdom. In Kabbalah, Hokhmah is the first sefirah and is considered the highest form of wisdom.

- **Hod:** Splendor. In Kabbalah, Hod is the eighth sefirah and is considered to be the highest expression of splendor.

- **Kabbalist:** A student or practitioner of Kabbalah.

- **Malchut:** The kingdom or realm. In Kabbalah, Malchut refers to the physical world, which is the lowest of the four spiritual worlds.

- **Merkabah:** In Kabbalah, the Merkabah is a symbol of our own journey to enlightenment. The Merkabah is the divine light vehicle used by the prophet Ezekiel to ascend to heaven. It is said that the Merkabah can help us attain our highest potential and connect with the divine.

- **Netzach:** Victory. In Kabbalah, Netzach is the seventh sefirah and is considered the highest expression of victory.

- **Olam HaBa:** The world to come, the afterlife. It is said that in Olam HaBa, we will be reunited with our loved ones who have passed on.

- **Olam HaZeh:** This world, the physical world. The lowest of the four spiritual worlds.

- **Pardes:** In Kabbalah, Pardes refers to the four levels of interpretation of scripture. The four levels are literal, allegorical, moral, and anagogical.

- **Raḥamim:** Compassion. In Kabbalah, Raḥamim is the ninth sefirah and is considered to be the highest expression of compassion.

- **Sefirot:** The 10 divine attributes or emanations of God used to create and sustain the universe.

- **Shekinah:** The divine presence of God. In Kabbalah, the Shekinah is often represented as a feminine aspect of God.

- **Shevirah:** The act of breaking or shattering. In Kabbalah, Shevirah refers to the moment when God created the universe by shattering the vessel that contained His infinite light. This act of divine creation resulted in the separation of the light from the darkness, which gave birth to the universe as we know it.

- **Tiferet:** Beauty. In Kabbalah, Tiferet is the sixth sefirah and is considered to be the highest expression of beauty.

- **Tikkun:** The process of repairing or mending. In Kabbalah, Tikkun refers to the process of repairing the world and restoring it to its original state of perfection.

- **Tzimtzum:** The act of self-contraction or withdrawal. In Kabbalah, Tzimtzum refers to the moment God withdrew His light to create the universe.

- **Yesod:** The foundation. In Kabbalah, Yesod is the ninth sefirah and is considered to be the foundation of all reality.

- **Zohar:** The central text of Kabbalah, which contains the mystical teachings of Rabbi Shimon bar Yochai.

Conclusion

As we have seen, Kabbalah is a mystical tradition with ancient roots. It teaches that we can access hidden knowledge and power by attaining a deep understanding of the divine nature of reality. Kabbalah also provides a powerful framework for understanding the human psyche and our place in the cosmos. Despite its great age, Kabbalah remains a living tradition that continues to evolve and grow. In recent years, it has experienced a resurgence of interest, with many people from all walks of life drawn to its wisdom.

In this guide on Kabbalah, we have explored some key concepts and practices that make up this tradition. We have looked at its history and how it has developed over time. We have also considered what it takes to become a Kabbalist and how Kabbalah can be used in our daily lives.

The Tree of Life is a central symbol, and we have spent some time exploring its meaning and significance. We have also looked at the Sephirot, the different levels of reality described by Kabbalah, and the role of the archangels in this tradition. From the Supernal Triad to the Ethical Triad and the Minor Arcana, Kabbalah provides us with a rich and detailed map of reality.

As we have seen, Kabbalah, complex and multifaceted, offers us a way to understand the world around us and where we fit in. By delving deeper into Kabbalah, we can better understand ourselves and the universe we inhabit. At the end of this guide, we explored some of the daily practices and rituals associated with Kabbalah. These are just a few of the many ways in which this tradition can enrich our lives.

Whether you are just beginning your exploration of Kabbalah or already well-versed in its teachings, we hope this guide has provided you with some valuable insights.

Kabbalah is a complex and rich tradition with much to offer to those willing to engage with it. We encourage you to continue your journey of discovery and wish you every success on your kabbalistic path. This informative guide has provided you with a brief introduction to Kabbalah. Hopefully, it has whetted your appetite to explore this rich and fascinating tradition further. There are many excellent books and resources available to help you on your journey of discovery. With an open mind and heart, Kabbalah can provide you with a lifetime of wisdom and insights. So, why not start your Kabbalistic journey today?

Here's another book by Silvia Hill that you might like

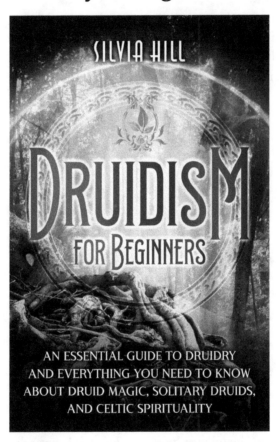

Free Bonus from Silvia Hill available for limited time

Hi Spirituality Lovers!

My name is Silvia Hill, and first off, I want to THANK YOU for reading my book.

Now you have a chance to join my exclusive spirituality email list so you can get the ebooks below for free as well as the potential to get more spirituality ebooks for free! Simply click the link below to join.

P.S. Remember that it's 100% free to join the list.

~~$27~~ FREE BONUSES

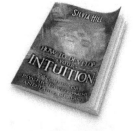

- 🖖 9 Types of Spirit Guides and How to Connect to Them
- 🖖 How to Develop Your Intuition: 7 Secrets for Psychic Development and Tarot Reading
- 🖖 Tarot Reading Secrets for Love, Career, and General Messages

Access your free bonuses here
https://livetolearn.lpages.co/kabbalah-paperback/

References

Kerstein, B. (2018). Kabbalah. World History Encyclopedia. https://www.worldhistory.org/Kabbalah/

My Jewish Learning. (2003, February 10). Kabbalah and mysticism 101. My Jewish Learning. https://www.myjewishlearning.com/article/Kabbalah-mysticism-101/

The Editors of Encyclopedia Britannica. (2022). Kabbala. In Encyclopedia Britannica.

What is Kabbalah? (2014). In Kabbalah: A Guide for The Perplexed. Continuum.

(N.d.-a). Labyrinthos.Co. https://labyrinthos.co/blogs/learn-tarot-with-labyrinthos-academy/the-tarot-and-the-tree-of-life-correspondences#:~:text=The%20nodes%20of%20the%20Tree,closer%20and%20closer%20to%20manifestation.

(N.d.-b). Chabad.org. https://www.chabad.org/library/article_cdo/aid/170308/jewish/What-is-Kabbalah.htm

Printed in the USA
CPSIA information can be obtained
at www.ICGtesting.com
LVHW021122040124
767941LV00007B/388